Cocktail

Cocktail

Over 200 of the best

hamlyn

First published in Great Britain in 2007 by Hamlyn,
a division of Octopus Publishing Group Ltd,
2–4 Heron Quays, London E14 4JP

Distributed in the United States and Canada by
Sterling Publishing Co., Inc., 387 Park Avenue South,
New York, NY 10016-8810

ISBN-13: 978-0-600-61570-5
ISBN-10: 0-600-61570-7

A CIP catalogue record for this book is available from
the British Library

Printed and bound in China

10 9 8 7 6 5 4 3 2 1

Notes

The measure that has been used in the recipes is based
on a bar jigger, which is 25 ml (1 fl oz). If preferred, a
different volume can be used, providing the proportions
are kept constant within a drink and suitable adjustments
are made to spoon measurements, where they occur.

Standard level spoon measurements are used throughout.
1 tablespoon = one 15 ml spoon
1 teaspoon = one 5 ml spoon
All recipes serve one unless otherwise specified.

Safety Note

The Department of Health advises that eggs should not
be consumed raw. This book contains recipes made with
raw eggs. It is prudent for more vulnerable people such as
pregnant and nursing mothers, invalids and the elderly to
avoid these recipes.

Contents

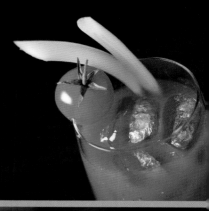

Introduction

The key to making successful cocktails is a combination of good techniques, an in-depth knowledge of drinks and ingredients and an eye for detail. A cocktail must look good and taste fantastic, and to achieve this every time you serve a drink can take years of practice. However, whether you are a novice mixologist or an accomplished bartender, you need to have the tools of the trade to hand and these should include a comprehensive reference book to keep behind the bar. Here you will find everything you need to create perfect cocktails every time. There are over 200 recipes, ranging from classic drinks to contemporary variations, as well as step-by-step instructions for mixing techniques, information about spirits and glasses and an extensive glossary of terms and ingredients.

The art of the cocktail

The cocktail has always been the glamorous drink of choice and has come to symbolize decadence, and it is the ideal drink for a night out to celebrate a special occasion. Bartenders in bars across the world continue the tradition of blending and mixing drinks, and the best among them make it look effortlessly easy. However, there is a definite art to cocktail creation, as well as a certain amount of science with regard to the composition of the drinks. You can't just throw together whatever spirits and liqueurs you happen to have in the cupboard – certain flavours naturally complement each other. When a bartender creates a new drink, it is probably the result of much experimentation and careful adjustment of the relative amounts of the different ingredients. That is why some of the great classic cocktails have survived until today and remain as popular as ever. Many are based on very simple combinations of everyday spirits and mixers, which generations of cocktail drinkers have enjoyed because the flavours work exceptionally well together. The *Dry Martini*, for example, with its ingredients consisting of vermouth and gin only, remains oft-requested in

bars today, its wonderful simplicity giving it a timeless appeal. While modern cocktails include all manner of unusual liqueurs, flavoured spirits and exotic fruit juices, it is rare to find a contemporary classic that will stand the test of time quite like this and other originals.

History in a glass

When you pour those first ingredients into the cocktail shaker, you will be following in the footsteps of bartenders who have been creating and serving mixed drinks, in one form or another, for well over 100 years. Although there is no definitive reference as to when the first cocktail was shaken or stirred, we know that spirits have been combined with mixers to create more interesting drinks for as long as alcohol has been enjoyed recreationally.

It must be said, though, that the glitzy and glamorous image of the cocktail is probably a relatively recent phenomenon. The idea of combining certain ingredients with alcohol is just as likely to have come about as a way in which to disguise the unpalatable taste of cheap spirits as through the pursuit of the ultimate taste experience in a glass. A prime example is the crude bootleg liquor of 1920s Prohibition America, which bartenders were able to transform with the imaginative use of different ingredient combinations by drawing on their pre-Prohibition experience when the cocktail had proved immensely popular. While Americans were drinking cocktails through necessity, however, Europeans were enjoying them through choice, heralding the heyday of the cocktail, with many classic drinks being created during this time in famous bars around the world.

Contemporary cocktails

The stories surrounding the now-legendary drinks, bars, bartenders and clientele have become steeped in modern-day folklore and have no doubt added to the wonderfully decadent image of the cocktail. As the wine bars of the 1980s slowly gave way to more sophisticated cocktail lounges, so people began to rediscover the versatility and appeal of cocktail drinking. Cocktails really do offer something for everyone, with drinks available that include every conceivable spirit or liqueur, and mixers ranging from exotic fruit to chocolate and everything in between. New drinks are being created all the time and successful beverages can put a bar on the map, with signature drinks earning the bartender considerable kudos.

Do try this at home

Many people will have enjoyed drinks while out for the evening or on holiday and want to re-create the experience at home, trying their hand at mixing their own cocktails. A cocktail party is a great idea for a social event at home, providing a fun focus for the evening and the perfect excuse for guests to dress up and make a special effort. If you are planning a cocktail party, don't be too ambitious about the number of drinks on offer – it is far better to prepare three or four drinks proficiently than attempt 20 and achieve less-than-successful results. Make sure you have the correct glasses for the cocktails you will be mixing (and plenty of them), as well as ample supplies of all the ingredients required, including a large quantity of ice. Also check that your equipment and tools for mixing the cocktails and preparing the decorations are in good working order and to hand. It is probably wise to discourage guests from making their own drinks. This does mean rather more work for you, but at least you will be in control of your bar – something every good bartender would advocate!

Tools of the trade

You don't need much specialist equipment to prepare cocktails, but there are a few essential tools that every decent bar should contain. If you are planning on creating drinks on a regular basis, it is well worth investing in the basics. Obviously, there are plenty more gadgets and cocktail-related tools available, but while some are useful, many will just end up languishing at the back of a drawer in your kitchen. The following is an overview of what you will need.

Shaker

This is an essential part of any bartender's toolkit, and if you are serious about mixing cocktails, you really should invest in a cocktail shaker. There are two basic types to choose from and it is a matter of personal preference as to which you buy.

Boston This is the professional bartender's choice of shaker. It comprises two parts: a Boston glass (a thick, sturdy, conical glass) and a shaking tin, which is basically a conical stainless steel container. The ice and all the other ingredients are put into the

Boston glass and the shaking tin positioned over the glass before shaking (see page 29). This shaker is traditionally used in conjunction with a hawthorne strainer.

Traditional This is the type of shaker that you are most likely to see on sale and as part of cocktail sets, but you will rarely see one of these when you are out for a drink in a bar. It is made up of three parts: the shaking tin, the strainer and the cap. The ice and all the other ingredients are added to the tin, then the strainer and cap are put in place to shake the cocktail (see page 29).

Boston shaker

Traditional shaker

Blender

Hawthorne strainer

Blender

Many people will already have one of these in their kitchen, but if you don't, it is probably not worth investing in one solely for making cocktails. However, this does depend on what your favourite tipple is, as blenders are indispensable when preparing frozen cocktails and smoothies. A blender or food processor will also prove useful if you need to make any concentrated fruit purées for use in drinks, although you could rub soft fruit through a non-metallic sieve instead. Despite being powerful, the blades of a blender are prone to blunting and general wear and tear, so you should only use crushed ice when creating cocktails (see page 22).

Hawthorne strainer

This strainer is used to strain a cocktail from a Boston shaker and is another accessory that is used by professional bartenders. A tea strainer and a steady hand will provide an acceptable alternative, although if you favour the Boston shaker, you will probably want to purchase a hawthorne strainer for your bar.

Fine strainer

This resembles a tea strainer. If a cocktail is shaken and served in a Martini (cocktail) glass, it is preferable to fine strain, or double strain, it to prevent all traces of puréed fruit and ice fragments from entering the glass. The fine strainer is often used in conjunction with the hawthorne strainer.

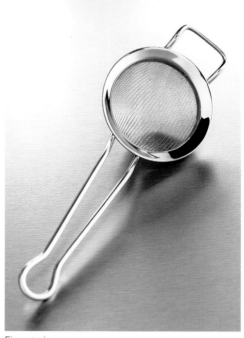
Fine strainer

Muddler

Bar spoon

Muddler

A muddler is similar to a pestle that is used in conjunction with a mortar. It is used to crush fruit, herbs and syrups in the bottom of a glass or cocktail shaker before making the rest of the cocktail (see page 28). These have become more commonplace in bars recently, due to the explosion in popularity of drinks such as the *Mojito* and the Brazilian *Caipirinha*.

Bar spoon

This is like a teaspoon with an exceedingly long handle so that it can reach the bottom of the tallest glass. It is a multi-purpose tool and is considered to be the bartender's best friend. It is used for stirring cocktails, layering drinks and other important tasks. Bar spoons usually have a spiral-shaped handle. This is handy for layering shots or adding a small amount of liquid to a drink, as it allows the liquid to be poured into the drink very slowly and evenly (see page 31).

Jiggers

Jiggers are small cylindrical metal containers that are used to ensure exact spirit measures and they generally come

in standard single or double spirit sizes. Cocktail making is all about achieving the correct proportions, and unless you are a highly trained bartender, you will not have mastered accurate free pouring, so measuring your ingredients is essential. Get this wrong and the balance of the drink will be distorted, which may well result in a sub-standard cocktail.

Jiggers

Bottle opener

neck of a spirit bottle to enable the spirit to flow in a controlled and measured manner.

Chopping board

A wooden chopping board is essential for preparing decorations and slicing fruit. Keep it wiped clean and close to hand.

Sharp knife

A good-quality knife will give you many years of service in the bar. A small knife, kept well sharpened, is best, as you will need to do some precision cutting if you want to make any elaborate decorations.

Bottle opener

Good bartenders should have a bottle opener on them at all times. The ideal design has two attachments – one for wine bottles and one for metal-capped bottles.

Pourers

Pourers are an essential part of any bartender's kit. They are inserted into the

Ice bucket and tongs

You will use up an enormous amount of ice when you are at the helm of a bar, so always make sure there is plenty available, whether in cubes, crushed or cracked (see page 22). An ice bucket and tongs is handy, but not essential. A clean sink or an empty ice-cream carton will suffice – as long as there is sufficient ice to make your drinks, it doesn't really matter how it is stored.

Pourers

Ice bucket and tongs

The drinks and their glasses

Although there are literally thousands of cocktails, most of them can be put into one of three categories: long, short or shot. This is a quick way of identifying drinks and also narrowing down your decision when you are ordering a cocktail. Indeed, many cocktail menus in bars will have these sub-headings. Unless you are a real connoisseur, you probably won't know all the drinks on the list, but you may well know whether you fancy a long drink or a quick shot.

Long drinks

As these cocktails will have a larger proportion of mixer than alcohol, they are a refreshing option that can be drunk with a straw. They will usually consist of one or two spirits or liqueurs topped up with a mixer or fruit juice, or a combination of both. Long drinks will often come with a decoration and frequently have an exotic-sounding name.

Short drinks

This is where terms such as 'straight up' and 'on the rocks' come into their own (see pages 154–157). Shorts are no-nonsense drinks that often comprise a single main spirit and a mixer. Many of these drinks will be prepared directly in the serving glass, although there are obviously many exceptions. For example, a *Harvey Wallbanger* requires vodka and orange juice to be shaken together in a cocktail shaker with ice before being poured into an ice-filled glass and topped with Galliano. This makes for a smooth drink that is extra cold. The higher alcohol ratio in short drinks means that they are designed for sipping rather than downing in one, and the inclusion of plenty of ice cubes results in the drink remaining chilled for the duration of drinking yet without it becoming diluted with water.

Shots

These are the ultimate party drinks. These miniature cocktails usually rely on spirits and liqueurs to make up most of their volume and the idea is to drink them in one hit. Certain spirits, most notably tequila, are sometimes served as a single measure in a shot glass, for a quick hit between longer drinks. The impressive layered shots test the steadiness of the bartender's hand (see page 31), but besides being aesthetically pleasing, the mixture of very different flavours and textures – for example, Kahlúa and Baileys Irish Cream combined with Grand Marnier in the *B-52* – results in a fantastic taste sensation when the shot is consumed.

Matching glasses with drinks

You can create the perfect cocktail, but it is only going to be as good as the glass you serve it in. Certain drinks work better in specific glasses, and the shape, thickness, size and appearance of the glass have been specially tailored to the type of drink it will contain. Can you imagine sipping Champagne from a tumbler or trying to swirl a brandy around a shot glass? If you don't have a good selection of glasses, you might want to consider which types of drinks you are going to prepare most frequently before you go shopping. The following directory should help.

Champagne flute Used for Champagne and Champagne cocktails, although these glasses are now available in a huge variety of shapes, with varying stem lengths, they should all have a narrow mouth. This ensures that the contents remain fizzy for as long as possible.

Champagne flute

Wine goblet Traditionally wine glasses with larger, broader bowls were used for bold red wines with bigger bouquets, and narrower glasses were used for lighter white wines. Wine glasses are rarely used for cocktails, with the odd exception, such as the *Pisco Sour*.

Wine goblet

Champagne saucer This is a fairly old-fashioned way of serving Champagne, made famous by the gigantic displays of 'Champagne pyramids' built throughout the 1980s. The fizz tends to disappear quickly in these wide-brimmed receptacles.

Champagne saucer

Martini (cocktail) glass The Martini glass is specially designed so that the hand does not warm the contents of the glass. The glass ignites debate among old-school bartenders, as anything served in it can be termed a Martini.

Martini (cocktail) glass

Margarita (coupette) glass This is the traditional glass for a *Margarita*, and its shape does justice to the often flamboyant variations on this classic cocktail. It has a wide rim, which is often frosted with salt (see page 26). It can also be used to serve *Daiquiris* and other fruit-based cocktails.

Margarita (coupette) glass

Rocks (old-fashioned) glass When whisky is served straight up or over ice, it should be served in this short, heavy-based glass. It is also ideal for muddled drinks, such as the *Caipirinha*, as it is robust and sturdy and can take the muddling of ingredients without cracking (see page 28).

Rocks (old-fashioned) glass

Highball glass This is the utility glass of the cocktail world, as all manner of concoctions may be served in a highball glass. These include everything from a straightforward *Gin and Tonic*, to *Mojitos*, *Breezes* and any long cocktail.

Highball glass

Shot glass Shot glasses often come in two sizes: a single and a double measured shot. They are used to serve potent drinks that are intended to be finished in a single mouthful. These range from tequila shots to the impressive, layered drinks such as the *B-52*.

Shot glass

Balloon (snifter) glass This bulbous glass is generally used for fine spirits, where the aromas are savoured as well as the taste, the shape of the glass allowing these aromas to be released without escaping. The glass may sometimes be warmed slightly to encourage the release of the aromas.

Balloon (snifter) glass

Boston glass This is the thick-bottomed, sturdy mixing glass that makes up the second half of a professional bartender's cocktail shaking kit (see page 10). Drinks are rarely served in these glasses, but they work well with long, fruit-based cocktails and smoothies.

Boston glass

Hurricane glass This glass is so-called because it resembles a hurricane lamp in shape. It is a less widely used glass, mostly seen in the beach bars of popular tourist destinations and usually used to serve long, creamy and often rum-based cocktails.

Hurricane glass

Toddy glass The toddy is another old-fashioned style of glass, which is generally used for serving hot drinks such as *Irish Coffee*. It is made of heat-resistant glass and is held by a handle, to prevent the hand from being burnt on the hot contents.

Toddy glass

The drinks and their glasses **17**

The spirits and their partners

Each of the main spirits, even those with a more subtle flavour such as gin, has a natural affinity with certain flavours, and it is from these complementary relationships that classic cocktails are born. Versatile vodka, however, is the exception.

Vodka

Vodka

Earlier versions of this popular spirit were actually made from rotting potatoes, so it will come as no surprise that vodka took a little while to gain a worldwide following! There is still fierce debate as to its country of origin, with the Poles and Russians both claiming to have invented the drink, but its manufacture can be traced all the way back to the ninth century. In those days, distillation methods were a little crude, to say the least, and the dubious taste of the spirit was often disguised by adding fruit, herbs or spices. Nowadays, vodka tends to be relatively free of any natural flavour. It is distilled from grain and is highly filtered to ensure that no trace of impurities remains in the final drink.

Many vodka brands now produce flavoured vodkas, with popular infusions including vanilla, raspberry, orange and lime. However, this is not a new invention by any means; there are some ancient Polish and Russian vodka houses that have been producing flavoured variations for centuries and these original infusions are still some of the best. Zubrowka Vodka (bison grass) and Krupnik Vodka (honey) are two outstanding examples.

Perfect partners Vodka is the subtlest of the spirits and the one that has introduced the age of 'mixology'. With its neutral character – often tasteless, odourless and colourless – it is infinitely mixable and works with a huge range of flavours, hence its use in literally hundreds of cocktails. Popular vodka partners are cranberry juice (used in the *Cosmopolitan*), tomato juice (*Bloody Mary*) and freshly squeezed lemon or lime (used in many Slings and Collins drinks). Then, of course, there is one of the world's favourite combinations – the Vodka and Tonic.

Rum

This Caribbean staple was originally developed in the 17th century as a way of using up the sugar cane that was left once the sugar had been produced. With a large transient population of sailors, this new liquor that was cheap to produce was an instant hit. It also quickly found its way over to Europe, hitching a ride back with the sugar. As with many spirits, rum is graded according to the length of time that it has been aged and ranges from light to

Rum

dark in appearance, the darker rums having been aged for anything up to 12 years. Rum has become a popular cocktail spirit; it has a reputation as a party drink and this can probably be attributed, in part at least, to its Caribbean ancestry, when many a sailor would enjoy a night out with a bottle of rum for company.

Perfect partners Rum is a wonderfully mixable spirit that comes in many forms and flavours. White rums are the easiest to pair up with mixers. They have a subtle flavour, which becomes more defined as you progress through gold and aged rums. Finally, dark rums have a very heavy and distinct flavour, which makes them difficult to mix successfully. Tropical flavours and rum work perfectly together, so why not try pineapple, coconut, guava or peach? In fact, there are very few fruits that cannot be made to work well in rum cocktails, if used with care and consideration. As with any cocktail, the key lies in experimenting with the sweet/sour balance of your drink and involving interesting flavours in moderation. Don't expect to get the end result spot-on first time – let the cocktail develop through trial and error, and sampling!

Gin

This is another clear, grain spirit and is essentially vodka steeped or infused with a number of botanicals, particularly juniper berries. Others commonly used are lemon rind, coriander, orange, almond, aniseed and fennel. Brands list the botanicals on the bottle to show the care taken to perfect the product's flavour.

Gin was first produced over 400 years ago in Holland and was initially developed as a medicine. However, it didn't take long for people to discover the inebriating properties of this new product and gin was eventually mass-produced and cheaply sold. This led to its undesirable reputation as 'mother's ruin', and resulted in many thousands of people becoming addicted to the spirit. It somehow managed to shake off this tarnished image and became popular with cocktail lovers in the 1920s.

Perfect partners When mixing gin, great care must be taken not to conflict with the

Gin

inherent flavours, but rather to encourage and complement them. Very clean, 'zingy' flavours work well, therefore citrus fruit and gin are great together, for example. Most fresh berries also have a natural affinity with gin, particular those with a relatively tart flavour such as raspberries and blackcurrants. However, one of the world's most popular cocktails is also one of the simplest: the *Gin and Tonic*. This should always be served very long and with plenty of ice.

Whisky

Whisky

As with vodka, the origins of whisky are hotly debated, with Scotland and Ireland both staking their claim as the birthplace of this spirit. Even the spelling is different: if you are sipping a Scotch, then it is 'whisky', but if you are in Ireland or the USA (or indeed any other country with the exception of Canada), then it is a 'whiskey' in your glass. As with many other spirits, historically it wasn't the refined drink we know today but a roughly distilled drink that purportedly cured various ailments. The ensuing years resulted in many improvements in distilling techniques, and although it is still produced from grain, modern whiskies have a much smoother texture and taste.

There are two main types of whisky: blended or unblended. The blended variety will include a combination of different whiskies, whereas unblended whiskies are just the single spirit.

Perfect partners The wide range of products within the whisky category makes it hard to generalize when discussing what works in whisky cocktails, maybe with the exception of cola and soda water. Whenever you are mixing drinks using this spirit, you should firstly identify the kind of whisky

you are dealing with and, secondly, you should try it neat before experimenting. Is it Scotch, bourbon, a single malt (there are many categories within this), blended, Irish, Canadian or Japanese? Then try and encourage an existing nuance of flavour that you notice within the liquor, maybe vanilla, coffee or chocolate – as with wine tasting, practice will help you to pick out certain flavour qualities. Everyone's taste sensations are different, so trust your own and use those as a guideline.

Tequila

Mexico's famous spirit is made from the blue agave plant and its origins can be traced back to the Aztecs. When the Spanish Conquistadors arrived in the 1500s, they were smitten with this unique spirit and began to set up distilleries to regulate the production of tequila. It made its way to America via the Conquistadors, where it found a ready market and swiftly gained in popularity. Traditionally, tequila was invariably drunk as a 'slammer', but the different grades of the spirit have recently begun to be appreciated more as a sipping drink and cocktail ingredient. Silver tequila is matured only briefly and

Tequila

liquid was sampled and found to be very drinkable, so plans were made to develop brandy under more controlled conditions.

Much brandy is still distilled from grapes, but there are many varieties that use other fruit as their base, with peach, apricot and apple being just some of the flavours.

Perfect partners Because brandy is a fruit distillate, it lends itself to blending with other fresh fruit and juices. However, many people would argue that fine brandy (such as VSOP and XO Cognacs) should not be mixed, as it is an unnecessary and expensive waste. The fact is that results will be just as delicious with a good VS, so it is definitely wise to save the better marques for drinking on their own. Brandy works well with nutty flavours like almond and hazelnut, as well as with dried fruit and berries such as apricots, raspberries and plums. Always blend brandy with care, as a good brandy can easily dominate a cocktail. The key is to try to complement and enhance its flavour.

remains clear, while gold tequila is aged for up to 11 months, allowing the flavour to develop and the colour to turn golden.

Perfect partners The intense and distinctive flavour of tequila means that making cocktails with this wonderful spirit is approached with great trepidation. It is most mixable with citrus and sour fruit as well as, surprisingly, savoury flavours such as tomato and ginger, as in the *Bloody Maria* and *El Diablo*. Once again, experimentation is the only way of discovering what works, so stick to the basics and try mixing tequila with your favourite flavours.

Brandy

As with rum, trading ships played a pivotal role in the history of brandy. It was by accident that brandy, as we know it, came about. When cargo ships were travelling the world gathering exotic fare, space was at a premium. Everything possible was done to squeeze a few more precious crates on board, so when someone worked out that if the water was extracted from wine they would be able to fit more on board, that is exactly what they did. The resultant

Brandy

Punch bowl and ladle

Mixers and other ingredients

If your bar is well stocked with the aforementioned spirits, you will be able to create hundreds of different cocktails. However, a cocktail is only a cocktail if the spirit is combined with other ingredients, and no bar would be complete without an extensive range of mixers. The list of potential spirit partners is endless, but there are certain drinks that you will use for a number of different cocktails, so it's well worth making sure you always have plenty to hand. Obviously, if you decide on certain cocktails that you think you will make regularly and that contain more unusual ingredients, it may be worth your while buying them as well.

Fruit juices Orange, lemon, lime, grapefruit, apple, cranberry and pineapple are some of the more commonly used fruit juices. Always use freshly squeezed citrus juices if possible. You can never have enough lemons and limes – many cocktails are decorated with citrus wheels or wedges (see page 23), so they won't go to waste. Choose good-quality, fresh varieties of the other fruit juices. Again, check individual recipes for other juices you might require.

Soda, tonic and lemonade These are often used to top up cocktails. You can buy individual servings in small cans in order to retain the fizz. This is more expensive than buying large bottles, so you need to work out how much you think you might need.

Additional mixers and flavourings

While some other ingredients may only be used in one or two cocktails, there are a few additional ones that you might like to add to your storecupboard. Tabasco sauce, Worcestershire sauce, Champagne, ginger beer, port and Angostura bitters are some of the ingredients that crop up in a number of cocktail recipes throughout the book.

Sugar syrup This is used in many cocktails, as it blends into a cold drink more quickly than ordinary sugar and gives it body. Sometimes called gomme syrup, syrup de gomme or just gomme, it is available ready made, but you can easily make your own. Put 4 tablespoons granulated sugar and 4 tablespoons water into a small saucepan and bring slowly to the boil, stirring to dissolve the sugar. Boil without stirring, for 1–2 minutes. Leave to cool. Store in a sterilized bottle in the refrigerator for up to 2 months.

Ice Ice cubes are mostly used for chilling ingredients when mixing cocktails, and widely used in glasses for serving. But crushed ice is also used for preparing and serving certain drinks, and is safer to use when blending ingredients in a blender (see page 11). To quickly crush ice, place the ice cubes in a strong polythene bag or between two clean tea towels and gently hit with a rolling pin until finely broken. Cracked ice, which is specified in some recipes, is made in the same way but not broken up so finely.

Mastering the art of garnishing

*The garnish or decoration adds the finishing touch to your creation. Classic cocktails often use traditional garnishes. For example, a **Dry Martini** is always served with a green olive. More contemporary drinks are decorated with a wide range of creations.*

Wheels

Any round fruit can be cut into cross-sections to create a wheel, such as kiwifruit, limes, lemons, oranges, apples and pears – just use your imagination and take your inspiration from the flavours in the cocktail.

1 Slice the fruit into cross-sections on a chopping board using a sharp paring knife.

2 Either place the wheel on the rim of the glass or float it on the surface of the drink.

Wedges

Lemons, limes, oranges and grapefruit can be cut into wedges. The wedge can be squeezed and dropped into the drink or served on the rim of the glass. Simply slide a sharp knife through the flesh so that it can balance on the rim.

1 Slice the fruit into halves, quarters, then eighths on a chopping board.

2 Use the wedge to decorate the rim of the glass or insert it into the cocktail.

Citrus twists

This imparts the flavour and aroma of a citrus fruit to a cocktail as well as decorating it. Twisting the strip of rind over the surface of the drink releases the citrus oils. Flame the rind before twisting to release even more flavour.

1 Pare a strip of rind from the fruit with a paring knife and remove all traces of pith.

2 Twist the strip of rind over the surface of the drink, then drop into the drink.

Citrus spirals

These decorations are entirely aesthetic. They look great draped around the rim of a glass or dropped inside.

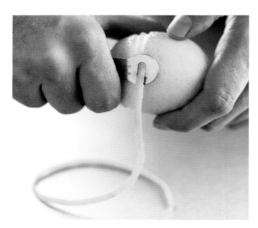

1 Cut a long strip of rind from a citrus fruit with a canelle knife.

2 Wind the rind around a cylindrical item, such as a bar spoon, glass swizzle stick or cocktail stick, depending on the size of the spiral required, to give it a spiral shape. Hold it in place for a few seconds to allow it to 'set' into the shape.

3 Lower the citrus spiral into the drink, or use it to decorate the rim of the glass.

Pineapple leaves

These decorations look fantastic with tropical-style cocktails such as the *Piña Colada* or any other cocktail that has pineapple amongst its ingredients. They are quick and easy to construct.

1 Slice the bottom from a pineapple leaf then slice the leaf in half from the base to halfway along its length.

2 Place the leaf upright on the edge of a highball or hurricane glass as a decoration.

Fruit kebabs

These enticing and delicious decorations are like miniature kebabs that can either be balanced on top of a glass or placed in the drink. Try a combination of berries, for example, in order of ascending size, a strawberry, a raspberry, a blueberry and a redcurrant. Other ideas include matching colours with the drink or using fruit that features as a flavouring in the cocktail.

1 Take a selection of small fruit, fruit pieces or berries and thread the fruit on to a cocktail stick.

2 Balance the fruit kebab on the edge of the cocktail glass to decorate.

Frosting glasses

Although not strictly a decoration, this effect does add to the final look of a drink. As with some other decorations, frosting can either perform a practical function, as in the *Margarita*, or a purely visual one. In general, glasses are either frosted with sugar or salt, but more unusual frostings can be used to complement flavours in cocktails, such as cocoa powder with a chocolate cocktail.

1 Dip the rim of the glass in a small saucer of lime or lemon juice, lightly beaten egg white or water.

2 Spread the desired frosting on a clean work surface or on a small plate or saucer. Place the glass on the frosting, twisting slightly to ensure you get an even coating.

3 Clean excess frosting from the inside of the glass using a lemon or lime wedge to prevent it from contaminating the cocktail.

4 Lastly, prepare the drink, being careful not to dislodge any of the frosting.

Herbs

Herb sprigs make very effective decorations. Mint looks and smells wonderful and is used to decorate a number of drinks, most notably the *Mojito*.

Novelty decorations

There are also a number of famous novelty decorations that are not as popular as they once were but can still, on the right occasion and with the right cocktail, look great. Paper umbrellas, plastic monkeys, even sparklers can certainly add a flourish to the appropriate theme. Use with care, though, as it is easy to get carried away with decorations and cross that fine line from the fun to the ridiculous!

Other ideas

The list of decorative possibilities is virtually endless and drinks can be decorated in many different ways, depending on the bartender. Take the great *Bloody Mary*, for example. Decorations for this particular cocktail can range from the more usual celery sticks, cucumber strips and cracked pepper to cherry tomatoes, basil leaves and even cocktail onions, prawns, grilled steak and quails' eggs! Get creative and try out your own ideas – you might just discover the next big craze.

Perfecting the craft

There are certain techniques that every good bartender should perfect before he or she is allowed to mix a drink for a customer, and the same goes for anyone serving cocktails at home. The following pages present step-by-step instructions and accompanying illustrations for these bartending techniques to help you to hone your craft and create perfect cocktails.

Muddling

Muddling is the technique used to bring the flavours out of fruit and herbs using a blunt tool called a muddler (see page 12). A famous example is the *Mojito*, where mint, sugar syrup and lime wedges are muddled in the bottom of a highball glass before the remaining ingredients are added.

1 Remove the mint leaves from their stems and put into the bottom of a highball glass. Add the sugar syrup and lime wedges. (See page 66 for quantities for making a *Mojito*.)

2 Hold the glass firmly with one hand and use the muddler to press down on the mint and lime wedges. Twist the muddler and press firmly in order to release the flavour of the mint and to break it down with the juice from the lime wedges.

3 Continue this process for about 30 seconds, then top up the glass with crushed ice. Add the remaining ingredients to the glass, as specified in the recipe.

Shaking

This is the most famous of all the cocktail-making processes and will probably be the technique you use most often, so it is important to get it just right. Shaking is used to mix ingredients quickly and thoroughly, and to chill the drink before serving. A *Cosmopolitan* is a famous shaken cocktail.

1 Half-fill the cocktail shaker or the Boston glass (if using a Boston shaker) with ice cubes (or the amount specified in the recipe), or add cracked or crushed ice.

2 If the recipe calls for a chilled glass, add a few ice cubes and some water to the glass and swirl them around before discarding.

3 Add the remaining ingredients to the shaker. Put on the strainer and cap or, if using a Boston shaker, place the shaking tin over the glass. Shake until condensation forms on the outside of the shaker. Use both hands to hold either end of the shaker and to prevent it from slipping from your grip.

4 The cocktail is then ready to be strained into the glass for serving by removing the cap but keeping the strainer in place. If using a Boston shaker, strain the drink through a hawthorne strainer (see page 11).

Stirring

'Shaken or stirred?' is the usual response from a bartender when a Martini is ordered, and despite James Bond's famously declared preference, Martinis are best served stirred, not shaken. A cocktail is prepared by stirring when it must maintain clarity yet also requires the ingredients to be mixed and chilled. This ensures that there is no fragmented ice or air bubbles throughout the drink. Some stirred cocktails will require the ingredients to be prepared in a mixing glass, then strained into the serving glass with a fine strainer, while others call for the drink to be prepared and stirred in the same glass.

1 Add the ingredients, in the order stated in the recipe, either to the mixing glass or the serving glass.

2 Using a bar spoon, either lightly or vigorously stir the drink, again according to the recipe. It is important to follow the recipe exactly, as some drinks will require just a slight blending of the ingredients and will not benefit from over-stirring.

3 Finish the drink with any decoration required and serve.

Layering

This is also referred to as *pousse café*. The technique involves a number of spirits and liqueurs being carefully layered, one by one, in a shot glass and the drink is then consumed in one mouthful. It is achieved by using the flat end of a bar spoon against the surface of each liquid and works because liquids have different densities, so some will be lighter than others and will therefore float on the layers beneath.

1 Pour the first liquid ingredient listed in the recipe into the shot glass, being careful not to allow any on the side of the glass.

2 Position the bar spoon in the centre of the glass with the rounded part of the spoon facing towards you. The spoon should be resting against the inside of the glass while also being in contact with the first liquid ingredient. Carefully and slowly pour the second liquid ingredient down the bar spoon so that it flows into the glass along the spoon and sits on top of the first liquid, creating a second layer.

3 Repeat with the third ingredient, then carefully remove the bar spoon.

Building

This is a very straightforward technique and one that should be mastered, which can be done with little practice. Building a cocktail is simply another way of describing the process of putting the ingredients together in the correct order, including any decoration – for example, filling a glass with crushed ice, pouring over a spirit and decorating with a herb sprig.

1 Have all the ingredients for the cocktail to hand before you begin. Chill the glass, if required, by swirling a few ice cubes around inside the glass and then discarding them.

2 Follow the recipe carefully, adding each ingredient in the specified order. Make sure you measure any spirits or liqueurs exactly. Prepare any decoration and add to the drink or glass before serving.

Blending

Frozen cocktails and smoothies are blended with ice in a blender until they are of a smooth consistency. A frozen *Daiquiri* or frozen *Margarita* is made using a virtually identical recipe to the unfrozen versions but with a scoop of crushed ice (see page 22) added to the blender before blending on high speed. Be careful not to add too much ice and consequently dilute the cocktail, so add a little at a time.

1 Make sure the blender is clean and to hand before you begin. Put a scoop of crushed ice into the blender and all the other ingredients specified in the recipe.

2 Blend on high speed until the mixture is of a slushy consistency. Pour into the appropriate glass and decorate according to the recipe.

Vodka

Bloody Mary
*The legendary 'Pete' Petoit, who worked at the famous Harry's Bar in Paris after the First World War, was the inventor of the **Bloody Mary**.*

ice cubes
2 measures vodka
1 dash lemon juice
Worcestershire sauce, to taste
tomato juice, to top up
½ teaspoon cayenne pepper
salt and pepper
tomato and celery stalks, to decorate

Put some ice cubes into a highball glass. Pour over the vodka and lemon juice, add Worcestershire sauce to taste and top up with tomato juice. Add the cayenne pepper and season to taste with salt and pepper. Stir to chill. Decorate with a tomato and celery stalks and serve. ▶

Bay Breeze
*This is a variation of the classic **Sea Breeze**. Here, pineapple juice is used to add a touch of sweetness that contrasts with the piquant flavour of cranberries.*

ice cubes
4 measures cranberry juice
2 measures vodka
2 measures pineapple juice
lime wedges (see page 23), to decorate

Fill a highball glass with ice cubes and pour over the cranberry juice. Pour the vodka and pineapple juice into a chilled cocktail shaker, shake well and gently pour over the cranberry juice and ice in the glass. Decorate with lime wedges and serve with long straws.

Dawa
The Swahili word 'dawa' means something between a medicine and a magic potion. It is traditionally served with a wooden masher to release more lime juice and adjust the flavour.

1 lime, quartered and thickly sliced
1 tablespoon thick honey
1 teaspoon caster sugar
2–3 ice cubes
2 measures vodka

Put the lime slices, honey and sugar into a rocks (old-fashioned) glass and muddle together (see page 28). Add the ice cubes and pour over the vodka, then serve.

Russian Spring Punch

For a slightly less decadent version of this drink, use a good-quality Cava instead of Champagne. You will still get the bubbles but it won't break the bank!

ice cubes
½ measure crème de cassis
1 measure freshly squeezed lemon juice
2 tablespoons sugar syrup (see page 22)
chilled Champagne, to top up
2 measures Absolut Vodka
lemon wedge (see page 23), and berries,
   to decorate

Fill a highball glass with ice cubes. Pour over the crème de cassis, lemon juice and sugar syrup, then pour in the chilled Champagne and the vodka together and stir (adding the vodka at the same time as the Champagne will prevent it from fizzing up). Decorate with a lemon wedge and berries, then serve. ▲

Vodka Sazerac
There's just a dash of Pernod in this cocktail but it's sufficient to impart the distinctive flavour to the finished drink without overwhelming it.

1 white sugar cube
2 drops Angostura bitters
3 drops Pernod
2–3 ice cubes
2 measures vodka
lemonade, to top up

Put the sugar cube into a rocks (old-fashioned) glass and shake the bitters on to it. Add the Pernod and swirl it around to coat the inside of the glass. Add the ice cubes and pour over the vodka. Top up with lemonade and stir lightly, then serve.

Screwdriver
A popular drink that is a simple but delicious combination of vodka and orange juice. As the ingredients are minimal it's important to use freshly squeezed juice.

2–3 ice cubes
1½ measures vodka
freshly squeezed orange juice, to top up

Put the ice cubes into a highball glass. Pour over the vodka, top up with orange juice and stir lightly, then serve.

Harvey Wallbanger
*This was named after a Californian surfer in the 1960s, who drank so many **Screwdrivers** with Galliano that he banged and bounced off the bar walls on his way out.*

6 ice cubes
1 measure vodka
3 measures freshly squeezed
   orange juice
1–2 teaspoons Galliano
orange wheels (see page 23),
   to decorate

Put half the ice cubes into a cocktail shaker and the remainder into a highball glass. Add the vodka and orange juice to the shaker and shake until a frost forms on the outside of the shaker. Strain over the ice in the glass. Float the Galliano on top (see page 31). Decorate with orange wheels and serve with straws.

Le Mans
Vodka and orange is combined again but here the orange is in the form of Cointreau. Soda water transforms this into a delicious long drink and the flavours become more subtle.

2–3 ice cubes, cracked (see page 22)
1 measure Cointreau
½ measure vodka
soda water, to top up
lemon wedge (see page 23), to decorate

Put the cracked ice into a highball glass. Pour over the Cointreau and vodka, stir and top up with soda water. Float a lemon wedge on top of the drink and serve. ▶

Illusion
Midori is a melon-flavoured liqueur that's produced in Mexico. However, the name relates to the liqueur's Japanese origins and it translates as 'green'.

ice cubes
2 measures vodka
½ measure Midori
½ measure triple sec
½ measure freshly squeezed lime juice
lemonade, to top up
fruit kebab (see page 25) of melon
    wedges, lemon wheels (see page 23)
    and cherries, to decorate

Half-fill a cocktail shaker with ice cubes and put some ice cubes into a large hurricane glass or a hollowed-out pineapple. Add the vodka, Midori, triple sec and lime juice to the shaker and shake until a frost forms on the outside of the shaker. Strain over the ice in the glass or pineapple shell. Top up with lemonade, stir and decorate with the fruit kebab. Serve with long straws.

Sea Breeze
*This refreshing contemporary classic is the tangier sister drink to **Bay Breeze**, made with pink grapefruit rather than pineapple juice.*

ice cubes
2 measures vodka
4 measures cranberry juice
2 measures freshly squeezed pink
    grapefruit juice
2 lime wedges (see page 23)

Put some ice cubes into a highball or hurricane glass. Pour over the vodka and fruit juices. Squeeze the lime wedges into the drink and stir lightly before serving.

Sex in the Dunes
Peach schnapps and Chambord are substituted for orange and cranberry juices in this variation of the popular Sex on the Beach cocktail.

ice cubes
1 measure vodka
1 measure peach schnapps
½ measure Chambord
1 measure pineapple juice
pineapple strips, to decorate

Half-fill a cocktail shaker with ice cubes and fill a rocks (old-fashioned) glass with ice cubes. Add all the remaining ingredients to the shaker and shake until a frost forms on the outside of the shaker. Strain over the ice in the glass. Decorate with pineapple strips and serve.

Cape Codder
This long drink gained in popularity with the vogue for cranberry juice. Cape Cod in Massachusetts is responsible for much of the USA's cranberry production.

ice cubes
2 measures vodka
4 measures cranberry juice
6 lime wedges (see page 23), to decorate

Fill a highball glass with ice cubes. Pour over the vodka and cranberry juice, then squeeze half the lime wedges into the drink. Stir well, decorate with the remaining lime wedges and serve with a straw, if you like.

Green Island Fragrance
There is a real citrus hit in this fruity cocktail. Temperature is important so make sure the cocktail is properly shaken, so that it chills well, before pouring into the glass.

ice cubes
1½ measures vodka
½ measure Midori
1 measure freshly squeezed lemon juice
1 measure pineapple juice
1 dash sugar syrup (see page 22)
1 lemon wedge (see page 23),
   to decorate

Half-fill a cocktail shaker with ice cubes and put some ice cubes into a highball glass. Add the vodka, Midori, fruit juices and sugar syrup to the shaker and shake until a frost forms on the outside of the shaker. Strain over the ice in the glass. Squeeze the lemon wedge into the drink, drop it in and serve with straws.

Bellini-tini

The Bellini was first created in Harry's Bar in Venice. The bartender named his drink after the Italian artist Giovanni Bellini.

4–5 ice cubes, cracked (see page 22)
2 measures vodka
½ measure peach schnapps
1 teaspoon peach juice
chilled Champagne, to top up
peach slices, to decorate

Put the cracked ice into a cocktail shaker. Add the vodka, schnapps and peach juice and shake until a frost forms on the outside of the shaker. Strain into a chilled Martini (cocktail) glass and top up with chilled Champagne. Decorate with peach slices and serve. ▲

Lemon Grass Collins
Another member of the extended 'Collins' family, the main ingredient of this drink is the unusual lemon grass vodka. This blends well with the ginger beer to give a spicy flavour.

crushed ice
2 measures lemon grass vodka
½ measure vanilla liqueur
1 dash freshly squeezed lemon juice
1 dash sugar syrup (see page 22)
ginger beer, to top up
lemon wedge (see page 23) and a stalk
   of lemon grass, to decorate

Fill a large highball glass with crushed ice. Build the vodka, vanilla liqueur, lemon juice and sugar syrup, one by one in order, over the ice. Stir, add more ice and top up with ginger beer. Decorate with a lemon wedge and a stalk of lemon grass and serve with long straws. ▶

Vodka Collins
The Collins takes its name from its creator, John Collins. He first mixed the drink in the early 19th century at Limmer's Hotel in London.

6 ice cubes
2 measures vodka
freshly squeezed juice of 1 lime
1 teaspoon caster sugar
soda water, to top up
lemon or lime wheels (see page 23) and
   a maraschino cherry, to decorate

Put half the ice cubes into a cocktail shaker. Add the vodka, lime juice and sugar and shake until a frost forms on the outside of the shaker. Strain into a large highball glass, add the remaining ice cubes and top up with soda water. Decorate with lemon or lime wheels and a maraschino cherry and serve.

Moscow Mule
This was invented in 1941 by an employee of a US drinks firm in conjunction with a Los Angeles bar owner who was overstocked with ginger beer.

3–4 ice cubes, cracked (see page 22)
2 measures vodka
freshly squeezed juice of 2 limes
ginger beer, to top up
lime or orange wheels (see page 23),
   to decorate

Put the cracked ice into a cocktail shaker. Add the vodka and lime juice and shake until a frost forms on the outside of the shaker. Pour, without straining, into a highball glass, top up with ginger beer and stir lightly. Decorate with lime or orange wheels and serve.

Parrot's Head Punch
There's a veritable explosion of fruit flavours in this exotic cocktail. A long refreshing drink that is best enjoyed whilst lounging in the sun.

ice cubes
1½ measures vodka
1 measure passion fruit liqueur
2 measures watermelon juice
1 measure cranberry juice
1½ measures freshly squeezed pink
    grapefruit juice
pink grapefruit wheel (see page 23),
    to decorate

Fill a hurricane glass with ice cubes. Build all the remaining ingredients, one by one in order, over the ice and decorate with a pink grapefruit wheel. Serve with long straws. ▸

White Russian
*This modern take on the **Black Russian** uses Tia Maria and cream to give the drink its distinctive colour and texture.*

6 ice cubes, cracked (see page 22)
1 measure vodka
1 measure Tia Maria
1 measure full-fat milk or double cream

Put half the cracked ice into a cocktail shaker and put the remaining cracked ice into a highball glass. Add all the remaining ingredients to the shaker and shake until a frost forms on the outside of the shaker. Strain over the ice in the glass. Serve with a straw.

Black Russian
This is the original cocktail, dating back to the 1950s. Nowadays, it is often served as a long drink, topped up with chilled cola.

4–6 ice cubes, cracked (see page 22)
2 measures vodka
1 measure Kahlúa
chocolate stick, to decorate (optional)

Put the cracked ice into a rocks (old-fashioned) glass. Pour over the vodka and Kahlúa and stir. Decorate with a chocolate stick, if you like, and serve.

Vodka Caipiroska
This is a vodka variation of the authentic Caipirinha cocktail, which traditionally features cachaça, a Brazilian spirit made from rum and sugar cane.

6 lime wedges (see page 23)
2 teaspoons soft light brown sugar
2 measures vodka
crushed ice

Put half the lime wedges, the sugar and vodka into a highball or rocks (old-fashioned) glass and muddle together (see page 28). Top up with crushed ice. Decorate with the remaining lime wedges and serve.

Vodka Daiquiri
The original Daiquiri came about at the beginning of the 20th century. It was apparently invented by a group of Americans who were working in Cuba at the time.

6 ice cubes, cracked (see page 22)
1 measure vodka
1 teaspoon caster sugar
freshly squeezed juice of ½ lime
  or lemon

Put the cracked ice into a cocktail shaker. Add all the remaining ingredients and shake until a frost forms on the outside of the shaker. Strain into a Martini (cocktail) glass and serve.

Vanilla Vodka Sour
The subtle, aromatic flavour of the vanilla vodka balances out the sour of the lemon juice and Angostura bitters in this unusual cocktail.

4–5 ice cubes
2 measures vanilla vodka
½ measure sugar syrup (see page 22)
1 egg white
1½ measures freshly squeezed
  lemon juice
3 drops Angostura bitters, to decorate

Put the ice cubes into a cocktail shaker. Add the vodka, sugar syrup, egg white and lemon juice and shake until a frost forms on the outside of the shaker. Pour, without straining, into a Martini (cocktail) glass and shake the Angostura bitters on top to decorate.

Rising Sun
The wonderful orange-red colour gives this cocktail its name. Place the pink grapefruit wheel at an angle on top of the drink to resemble the rising sun.

ice cubes
2 measures vodka
2 teaspoons passion fruit syrup
3 measures freshly squeezed
   grapefruit juice
pink grapefruit wheel (see page 23),
   to decorate

Half-fill a cocktail shaker with ice cubes and put 6–8 ice cubes into a rocks (old-fashioned) glass. Add all the remaining ingredients to the shaker and shake until a frost forms on the outside of the shaker. Strain over the ice in the glass. Decorate with a pink grapefruit wheel and serve. ▲

Kiwi Caipiroska
*The addition of kiwifruit gives the **Vodka Caipiroska** a delicious fruity twist.*

½ kiwifruit, peeled
½ lime, cut into wedges (see page 23)
2 teaspoons sugar syrup (see page 22)
crushed ice
2 measures vodka
2 teaspoons kiwifruit schnapps

Put the kiwifruit, lime wedges and sugar syrup into a rocks (old-fashioned) glass and muddle together (see page 28). Fill the glass with crushed ice, pour over the vodka and stir. Add more ice, then drizzle the schnapps over the surface. ▶

Vodkatini
A simple combination of ingredients results in a crisp, clean flavour that is complemented by the olives.

5–6 ice cubes
3 measures chilled vodka
½ measure Noilly Prat
olives, to decorate

Put the ice cubes into a mixing glass. Pour over the vodka and Noilly Prat and stir vigorously and evenly without splashing. Strain into a chilled Martini (cocktail) glass. Decorate with olives and serve.

Flower Power Sour
This is an unusual, fresh and fragrant sour, made with vodka flavoured with Mandarine Napoléon, a liqueur infused with mandarin rind, and elderflower cordial.

ice cubes
1½ measures Absolut Mandarin Vodka
½ measure Mandarine Napoléon
2 teaspoons elderflower cordial
2 teaspoons sugar syrup (see page 22)
1 measure freshly squeezed lemon juice
orange rind spiral (see page 24),
   to decorate

Half-fill a cocktail shaker with ice cubes and fill a rocks (old-fashioned) glass with ice cubes. Add all the remaining ingredients to the shaker and shake until a frost forms on the outside of the shaker. Strain over the ice in the glass. Decorate with an orange rind spiral and serve.

Kurant Blush
The name of this drink derives from the Absolut Kurant Vodka it contains. Crème de fraise and cranberry juice help to continue the fruity theme, whilst a redcurrant decoration finishes the drink.

ice cubes
1½ measures Absolut Kurant Vodka
½ measure crème de fraise
1 measure cranberry juice
2 lime wedges (see page 23)
redcurrant, to decorate

Half-fill a cocktail shaker with ice cubes. Add all the remaining ingredients and shake until a frost forms on the outside of the shaker. Fine or double strain (see page 11) into a chilled Martini (cocktail) glass. Decorate with a redcurrant on a cocktail stick and serve.

Iceberg
Pernod is probably the best known of the pastis – French aniseed-flavoured spirits that are drunk as an aperitif.

4–6 ice cubes
1½ measures vodka
1 dash Pernod

Put the ice cubes into a rocks (old-fashioned) glass. Pour over the vodka and add the Pernod, then serve.

Apple Martini
Martinis come in every possible guise and this variation uses apple as its inspiration. The warming taste of apple schnapps is complemented by ground cinnamon.

ice cubes
2 measures vodka
1 measure apple schnapps
1 tablespoon apple purée
1 dash freshly squeezed lime juice
pinch of ground cinnamon
red apple wedges, to decorate

Half-fill a cocktail shaker with ice cubes. Add all the remaining ingredients and shake until a frost forms on the outside of the shaker. Fine or double strain (see page 11) into a chilled Martini (cocktail) glass. Decorate with red apple wedges and serve.

Glamour Martini
The vibrant colour of this aesthetically pleasing cocktail means that it more than lives up to its name. An orange rind twist adds the finishing touch.

ice cubes
1½ measures vodka
½ measure cherry brandy
2 measures freshly squeezed blood
    orange juice
½ measure freshly squeezed lime juice
orange rind twist (see page 24),
    to decorate

Half-fill a cocktail shaker with ice cubes. Add all the remaining ingredients and shake until a frost forms on the outside of the shaker. Strain into a chilled Martini (cocktail) glass. Decorate with an orange rind twist and serve. ▲

Cosmopolitan
*Many people make claim on being the inventor of the **Cosmopolitan**; however, it is a relatively recent cocktail that has become something of a classic already.*

6 ice cubes, cracked (see page 22)
1 measure vodka
½ measure Cointreau
1 measure cranberry juice
freshly squeezed juice of ½ lime
orange rind twist, to decorate

Put the cracked ice into a cocktail shaker. Add all the remaining ingredients and shake until a frost forms on the outside of the shaker. Strain into a chilled Martini (cocktail) glass. Decorate with an orange rind twist and serve. ▶

Valentine Martini
The pink hue of this drink gives it its romantic name. This is achieved by the addition of raspberry vodka, which also adds a sweet flavour.

ice cubes
2 measures raspberry vodka
6 raspberries, plus 2 extra to decorate
½ measure freshly squeezed lime juice
1 dash sugar syrup (see page 22)
lime rind twist (see page 24),
   to decorate

Half-fill a cocktail shaker with ice cubes. Add all the remaining ingredients and shake until a frost forms on the outside of the shaker. Fine or double strain (see page 11) into a chilled Martini (cocktail) glass. Decorate with the extra raspberries on a cocktail stick and a lime rind twist and serve.

Watermelon Martini
Watermelon, passion fruit and cranberry combine here to make a refreshingly fruity cocktail. Use a fine strainer to create a clearer drink.

ice cubes
1 lime wedge (see page 23)
4 watermelon chunks, plus a wedge
   to decorate
1½ measures vodka
½ measure passion fruit liqueur
1 dash cranberry juice

Half-fill a cocktail shaker with ice cubes. Squeeze the lime wedge into the shaker, add all the remaining ingredients and shake until a frost forms on the outside of the shaker. Fine or double strain (see page 11) into a chilled Martini (cocktail) glass. Decorate with a watermelon wedge and serve.

Kitsch Revolt

The strawberry purée for this cocktail can be bought ready made or prepared by puréeing hulled ripe strawberries in a blender or food processor or rubbing through a non-metallic sieve.

ice cubes
1 measure Absolut Kurant Vodka
½ measure strawberry purée
5 measures chilled Champagne
strawberry, to decorate

Half-fill a cocktail shaker with ice cubes. Add the vodka and strawberry purée and shake briefly to mix. Strain into a Martini (cocktail) glass. Top up with the chilled Champagne and stir. Decorate with a strawberry, then serve. ◄

Swallow Dive

Krupnik Vodka is made to a recipe that was developed hundreds of years ago by Bénédictine monks. Its popularity has spread from its native Poland and Lithuania.

ice cubes
crushed ice
1 measure honey vodka, such as
   Krupnik Vodka
1 measure Chambord
1 measure freshly squeezed lime juice
4 raspberries, plus 2 extra to decorate

Half-fill a cocktail shaker with ice cubes and put some crushed ice into a rocks (old-fashioned) glass. Add all the remaining ingredients to the shaker and shake until a frost forms on the outside of the shaker. Strain over the ice in the glass. Top up with more crushed ice. Decorate with the extra raspberries and serve.

Vodka Grasshopper

Crème de menthe gives this cocktail its distinctive name and colour. Mint meets its perfect partner, chocolate, with the addition of crème de cacao.

crushed ice
1½ measures vodka
1½ measures green crème de menthe
1½ measures white crème de cacao

Half-fill a cocktail shaker with crushed ice. Add all the remaining ingredients and shake until a frost forms on the outside of the shaker. Strain into a chilled Martini (cocktail) glass and serve.

Gingersnap
This is a light drink that would make a good aperitif. The simplicity of the ingredients means there's no need for a decoration.

2–3 ice cubes
3 measures vodka
1 measure ginger wine
soda water, to top up

Put the ice cubes into a rocks (old-fashioned) glass. Pour over the vodka and ginger wine and stir lightly. Top up with soda water and serve.

Katinka
Mint is used as a decoration for many drinks. If you are a cocktail connoisseur, why not consider growing your own?

ice cubes
1½ measures vodka
1 measure apricot brandy
2 teaspoons freshly squeezed lime juice
mint sprig, to decorate

Half-fill a cocktail shaker with ice cubes. Add all the remaining ingredients and shake until a frost forms on the outside of the shaker. Strain into a Martini (cocktail) glass. Decorate with a mint sprig and serve.

Xantippe
Chartreuse is a herb-based liqueur named after a Carthusian monastery near Grenoble in France where it was first made. Yellow Chartreuse has a lower alcohol content than Green Chartreuse.

4–5 ice cubes
1 measure cherry brandy
1 measure Yellow Chartreuse
2 measures vodka

Put the ice cubes into a mixing glass. Pour over the cherry brandy, Chartreuse and vodka and stir vigorously. Strain into a chilled Martini (cocktail) glass, then serve.

New Day *Sip this cocktail slowly as the alcohol content is quite high!*
The freshly squeezed orange juice complements the Calvados and adds extra
texture to the drink.

4–5 ice cubes
3 measures vodka
1 measure Calvados
1 measure apricot brandy
freshly squeezed juice of ½ orange
orange wedge (see page 23), to decorate

Put the ice cubes into a cocktail shaker. Add all
the remaining ingredients and shake until a
frost forms on the outside of the shaker. Strain
into a rocks (old-fashioned) glass, decorate
with an orange wedge and serve. ▲

Decatini
This is an apt name for a truly luxurious cocktail that will appeal especially to chocoholics. Raspberries, cherry purée, chocolate and cream are blended to perfection.

ice cubes

2 measures raspberry vodka

½ measure chocolate syrup, plus extra
   to decorate

½ measure double cream

1 measure morello cherry purée

Half-fill a cocktail shaker with ice cubes. Add the vodka, chocolate syrup and half the cream and shake until a frost forms on the outside of the shaker. Strain into a chilled Martini (cocktail) glass. Wash out the shaker, then add the cherry purée and the remaining cream and shake briefly to mix. Float the cherry liquid over the chocolate liquid in the glass (see page 31). Decorate with a swirl of chocolate syrup and serve. ▶

White Elephant
It's not difficult to see why this drink got its name. White crème de cacao, cream and milk create a rich, creamy texture.

ice cubes

1½ measures vodka

1 measure white crème de cacao

1 measure single cream

½ measure full-fat milk

Half-fill a cocktail shaker with ice cubes. Add all the remaining ingredients and shake until a frost forms on the outside of the shaker. Strain into a chilled Martini (cocktail) glass and serve.

Vanilla Skyy
Skyy vodka contains very few impurities as the brand pioneered the multiple distillation and filtration process in 1992. This gives the vodka a particularly clean, crisp quality.

ice cubes

2 teaspoons dry vermouth

1 measure vanilla vodka

1 measure Skyy vodka

½ measure apple schnapps

apple chunks frozen in apple juice ice
   cubes, to decorate

Fill a mixing glass with ice cubes. Add the vermouth, stir and strain, discarding the excess vermouth and leaving the flavoured ice. Add the vodkas and the schnapps, stir and strain into a chilled Martini (cocktail) glass. Decorate with the apple-chunk ice cubes and serve.

Blackberry Martini

The powerful flavours for this Martini are provided by Absolut Kurant, a blackcurrant-flavoured vodka, and crème de mûre, a blackberry liqueur.

2 measures Absolut Kurant Vodka
1 measure crème de mûre
ice cubes
blackberry, to decorate

Put the vodka and crème de mûre into a mixing glass, add some ice cubes and stir well. Strain into a chilled Martini (cocktail) glass. Decorate with a single blackberry and serve.

Polish Martini

This is a wonderfully mellow Martini. It is made with three different types of Polish vodka, with bison grass, honey and traditional flavours.

ice cubes
1 measure Zubrowka Vodka
1 measure Krupnik Vodka
1 measure Wyborowa Vodka
   (standard Polish)
1 measure apple juice
lemon rind twist (see page 24),
   to decorate

Put some ice cubes into a mixing glass. Pour over the three vodkas and the apple juice and stir well. Strain into a chilled Martini (cocktail) glass. Decorate with a lemon rind twist and serve.

Kiwi-tini

As well as tasting great, this cocktail is aesthetically pleasing with its bright green colour and the dots of the kiwi pips floating throughout.

½ kiwifruit, peeled
¼ measure sugar syrup (see page 22)
ice cubes
2 measures vodka
½ measure kiwifruit schnapps
kiwifruit wheel (see page 23),
   to decorate

Put the kiwifruit and sugar syrup into a mixing glass and muddle together (see page 28). Half-fill a cocktail shaker with ice cubes. Add the kiwifruit mixture and all the remaining ingredients and shake until a frost forms on the outside of the shaker. Strain into a chilled Martini (cocktail) glass. Fine or double strain (see page 11) if you want to remove all the kiwifruit pips, although they look good left in. Decorate with a kiwifruit wheel and serve.

Horizon
Zubrowka is a Polish vodka that's made from rye grain and bison grass. It has recently gained an increased following amongst drinkers and bartenders.

ice cubes
1½ measures Zubrowka Vodka
½ measure Xante pear liqueur
1 measure pressed apple juice
1 teaspoon passion fruit liqueur
1 dash lemon juice
pared lemon rind, to decorate

Half-fill a cocktail shaker with ice cubes. Add all the remaining ingredients and shake until a frost forms on the outside of the shaker. Fine or double strain (see page 11) into a chilled Martini (cocktail) glass. Decorate with pared lemon rind and serve. ▲

Pillow Talk
What could be more enticing than strawberries and chocolate? Try this shot and you will know the answer!

½ measure chilled strawberry vodka
½ measure Mozart white
   chocolate liqueur
1 squirt aerosol cream

Using a bar spoon, carefully layer the vodka and white chocolate liqueur in a shot glass (see page 31). Add a squirt of aerosol cream, then serve. ▶

Kamikaze
This is a shot with a real zing. The kick of the lime juice will take effect immediately if you slam this like a tequila.

6 ice cubes, cracked (see page 22)
½ measure vodka
½ measure triple sec
½ measure freshly squeezed lime juice

Put the cracked ice into a cocktail shaker. Add all the remaining ingredients and shake until a frost forms on the outside of the shaker. Strain into a shot glass and serve.

Rock Chick
Blackcurrant and peach flavours are combined with a dash of fresh lime to cut through the sweetness in this delicious shot.

ice cubes
1 measure Absolut Kurant Vodka
1 dash peach schnapps
1 dash freshly squeezed lime juice

Half-fill a cocktail shaker with ice cubes. Add all the remaining ingredients and shake briefly to mix. Strain into a shot glass and serve.

Lemon Drop
Here is another citrus hit with the lemon coming threefold: lemon vodka, Limoncello and lemon juice. Lime cordial adds the perfect finishing touch.

ice cubes
¾ measure lemon vodka
¾ measure Limoncello
1 dash freshly squeezed lemon juice
1 dash lime cordial

Half-fill a cocktail shaker with ice cubes. Add all the remaining ingredients and shake briefly to mix. Strain into a shot glass and serve.

Bloody Simple
Pepper or chilli vodka and Tabasco sauce give this shot a fiery aftertaste, and a peppery tomato wedge adds fuel to the fire.

1 measure chilled pepper or chilli vodka
2–3 drops Tabasco sauce
pepper
celery salt
1 tomato wedge

Pour the vodka into a shot glass, then add the Tabasco sauce. Mix some pepper and celery salt together on a small saucer. Dip the tomato wedge into the pepper and salt mixture to lightly coat, then eat after drinking the shot.

Mint Zing Ting
This fresh little number has a green theme with its apple, lime and mint flavours, and a cucumber finish.

1 lime wedge (see page 23)
2 mint leaves
1 dash sugar syrup (see page 22)
ice cubes
1 measure apple-soaked vodka
cucumber strip, to decorate

Put the lime wedge, mint and sugar syrup into a cocktail shaker and muddle together (see page 28). Half-fill the shaker with ice cubes, add the vodka and shake until a frost forms on the outside of the shaker. Strain into a chilled shot glass. Decorate with a cucumber strip and serve.

Purple Haze
Chambord is a raspberry-flavoured liqueur that takes its name from the Château de Chambord. The liqueur's other ingredients include honey and vanilla.

ice cubes

1 measure vodka

1 dash Cointreau

1 dash freshly squeezed lemon juice

1 dash Chambord

Half-fill a cocktail shaker with ice cubes. Add the vodka, Cointreau and lemon juice and shake briefly to mix. Strain into a shot glass. Slowly add the Chambord – this will then settle towards the bottom of the drink – and serve. ▲

Rum

Mojito
This is a cooling, effervescent cocktail born – thanks to Prohibition – amid Cuba's thriving international bar culture. It probably derived from the Mint Julep.

**12 mint leaves, plus an extra sprig
  to decorate
½ measure sugar syrup (see page 22)
4 lime wedges (see page 23)
crushed ice
2 measures white rum
soda water, to top up**

Put the mint, sugar syrup and lime wedges into a highball glass and muddle together (see page 28). Fill the glass with crushed ice, pour over the rum and stir. Top up with soda water. Decorate with a mint sprig and serve with straws. ▶

Pink Mojito
Crushed raspberries, Chambord and cranberry juice give a distinctive colour to this variation of the classic Mojito. A great summertime drink.

**6 mint leaves, plus an extra sprig
  to decorate
½ lime, cut into wedges (see page 23)
2 teaspoons sugar syrup (see page 22)
3 raspberries
crushed ice
1½ measures white rum
½ measure Chambord
cranberry juice, to top up**

Put the mint leaves, lime wedges, sugar syrup and raspberries into a highball glass and muddle together (see page 28). Add some crushed ice, then pour over the rum and Chambord. Stir well and top up with cranberry juice. Decorate with a mint sprig and serve.

Pineapple Mojito
Another fruity take on the original, this time using pineapple to create a lovely sweet flavour.

**6 mint leaves, plus an extra sprig
  to decorate
4 pineapple chunks, plus a wedge
  to decorate
2 teaspoons soft light brown sugar
ice cubes
crushed ice
2 measures golden rum, such as Havana
  Club 3-year-old
pineapple juice, to top up**

Put the mint leaves, pineapple chunks and sugar into a cocktail shaker and muddle together (see page 28). Half-fill the shaker with ice cubes and fill a highball glass with crushed ice. Add the rum to the shaker and shake until a frost forms on the outside of the shaker. Strain over the ice in the glass. Top up with pineapple juice and stir. Decorate with a pineapple wedge and a mint sprig and serve.

Cuba Libre

Legend has it that this famous cocktail was invented in Cuba in the 1800s as a way for soldiers to get away with drinking alcohol — the cola and lime apparently disguised the rum.

ice cubes
2 measures golden rum, such as Havana
  Club 3-year-old
freshly squeezed juice of ½ lime
cola, to top up
lime wedges (see page 23), to decorate

Fill a rocks (old-fashioned) or highball glass with ice cubes. Pour over the rum and lime juice and stir. Top up with cola. Decorate with lime wedges and serve with straws. ▲

Apple-soaked Mojito *Apple and mint make a really refreshing combination, and this drink is perfect for a summer party.*

8 mint leaves, plus an extra sprig
  to decorate
½ lime, cut into wedges (see page 23)
2 teaspoons sugar syrup (see page 22)
crushed ice
2 measures golden rum, such as Havana
  Club 3-year-old
1 measure apple juice
red apple slices, to decorate

Put the mint leaves, lime wedges and sugar syrup into a cocktail shaker and muddle together (see page 28). Fill a highball glass with crushed ice. Add the rum to the shaker and shake well (do not add ice to the shaker). Strain over the ice in the glass and top up with the apple juice. Decorate with a mint sprig and red apple slices and serve.

Monoloco Zombie *This is a seriously well-stocked cocktail with two measures of different rums, brandy and orange curaçao, as well as three fruit juices. Another half measure of rum finishes off the drink.*

ice cubes
1 measure white rum
1 measure Wood's Navy Rum
½ measure apricot brandy
½ measure orange curaçao
2 measures freshly squeezed
  orange juice
2 measures pineapple juice
½ measure freshly squeezed lime juice
1 dash grenadine
½ measure overproof rum
pineapple wedges, to decorate

Half-fill a cocktail shaker with ice cubes and put some ice cubes into a large hurricane glass. Add all the remaining ingredients, except the overproof rum, to the shaker and shake until a frost forms on the outside of the shaker. Strain over the ice in the glass. Top with the overproof rum. Decorate with pineapple wedges and serve.

Mai Tai *This cocktail contains orgeat syrup, a sweet syrup that is made from almonds, sugar and rose or orange-flower water and is non-alcoholic.*

ice cubes
crushed ice
2 measures golden rum
½ measure orange curaçao
½ measure orgeat syrup
freshly squeezed juice of 1 lime
2 teaspoons Wood's Navy Rum
lime rind spiral (see page 24) and mint
  sprig, to decorate

Half-fill a cocktail shaker with ice cubes and put some crushed ice into a rocks (old-fashioned) glass. Add the golden rum, curaçao, orgeat syrup and lime juice to the shaker and shake until a frost forms on the outside of the shaker. Strain over the ice in the glass. Float the Navy Rum on top (see page 31). Decorate with a lime rind spiral and a mint sprig and serve.

The Papa Doble
This was Ernest Hemingway's famed tipple. It can be sweetened with half a measure of sugar syrup and downscaled to two measures of rum, if desired.

1 scoop crushed ice
3 measures white rum
½ measure maraschino
1 measure freshly squeezed lime juice
1½ measures freshly squeezed
   grapefruit juice
grapefruit wedge (see page 23),
   to decorate

Put the crushed ice into a blender. Add all the remaining ingredients and blend on high speed until smooth. Pour into a highball glass. Decorate with a grapefruit wedge and serve with straws. ▶

Spiced Mule
The subtle flavours of the spiced rum give real warmth to this drink. It's designed to be shared and would make a good tipple for winter parties.

Serves 6
ice cubes
8 measures spiced rum
2 measures freshly squeezed lime juice
2 measures sugar syrup (see page 22)
1 litre (1¾ pints) ginger beer, to top up
lime wedges (see page 23), to decorate

Half-fill the cocktail shaker with ice cubes and fill highball glasses with ice cubes. Add the rum, lime juice and sugar syrup to the shaker and shake until a frost forms on the outside of the shaker. Pour into a large glass jug. Add more ice and top with ginger beer while stirring. Pour over the ice in the glasses, decorate with lime wedges and serve.

Planter's Punch
This was created by Fred L Myers in the late 19th century. For a modern fruity version, substitute pineapple juice for the water.

ice cubes
2 measures Myer's Jamaican Planter's
   Punch Rum
4 drops Angostura bitters
½ measure freshly squeezed lime juice
2 measures iced water
1 measure sugar syrup (see page 22)
orange and lime wheels (see page 23),
   to decorate

Half-fill a cocktail shaker with ice cubes and fill a highball glass with ice cubes. Add all the remaining ingredients to the shaker and shake until a frost forms on the outside of the shaker. Strain over the ice in the glass. Decorate with orange and lime wheels and serve.

Blue Hawaiian
Blue curaçao is made from dried orange peel and is bright blue in hue as a result of added colouring.

1 scoop crushed ice
1 measure white rum
½ measure blue curaçao
2 measures pineapple juice
1 measure coconut cream
pineapple wedge, to decorate

Put the crushed ice into a blender. Add all the remaining ingredients and blend on high speed for 20–30 seconds. Pour into a chilled Martini (cocktail) glass. Decorate with a pineapple wedge and serve.

Cuban Breeze
You should invest in a good-quality aged rum to create a beautifully mellow drink.

ice cubes
3 measures cranberry juice
2 measures golden rum, such as Havana
   Club 3-year-old
2 measures freshly squeezed
   grapefruit juice
lime wedges (see page 23), to decorate

Fill a highball glass with ice cubes and pour over the cranberry juice. Half-fill a cocktail shaker with ice cubes. Add the rum and grapefruit juice and shake until a frost forms on the outside of the shaker. Strain over the cranberry juice and ice in the glass. Decorate with lime wedges and serve.

Clem the Cuban
Apple schnapps and rum make an unusual partnership in this muddled drink. It's served as a shot so down it in one.

1 dash apple schnapps
1 mint sprig
2 lime wedges (see page 23)
1 measure golden rum, such as Havana
   Club 3-year-old
1 scoop crushed ice

Put the schnapps, mint sprig and lime wedges into a cocktail shaker and muddle together (see page 28). Add the rum and crushed ice and shake very briefly to mix. Fine or double strain (see page 11) into a shot glass and serve.

Piña Colada
This world-famous cocktail was created by a bartender in Puerto Rico in 1957. It is a homage to the exotic flavours of the country.

1 scoop crushed ice
2 measures white rum
2 teaspoons freshly squeezed lime juice
2 measures coconut cream
2 measures pineapple juice
1 scoop vanilla ice cream
pineapple leaf (see page 25), to decorate

Put the crushed ice into a blender. Add all the remaining ingredients and blend on high speed for 20–30 seconds. Pour into a highball glass, decorate with a pineapple leaf and serve. ▲

Rum Crusta
As well as brandy, a Crusta can be made with gin, rum or whisky. This one combines the rich flavour of dark rum with the zesty tang of Cointreau.

lime wedge (see page 23)
caster sugar
crushed ice
ice cubes
2 measures dark rum
1 measure Cointreau
2 teaspoons maraschino
2 teaspoons freshly squeezed lime juice
grape kebab (see page 25), to decorate

Moisten the rim of a rocks (old-fashioned) glass with the lime wedge and frost with the sugar (see page 26). Fill the glass with crushed ice and half-fill a cocktail shaker with ice cubes. Add all the remaining ingredients to the shaker and shake until a frost forms on the outside of the shaker. Strain over the ice in the glass. Decorate with a grape kebab and serve. ▶

Hummingbird
White and dark rums are combined with whisky, fruit juice and cola in this long drink bursting with character.

4–5 ice cubes, crushed (see page 22)
1 measure dark rum
1 measure white rum
1 measure Southern Comfort
1 measure freshly squeezed orange juice
cola, to top up
orange wheel (see page 23), to decorate

Put the crushed ice into a cocktail shaker. Add the rums, Southern Comfort and orange juice and shake until a frost forms on the outside of the shaker. Strain into a highball glass and top up with cola. Decorate with an orange wheel and serve with a straw.

Havana Beach
Here's another cocktail with Cuban connections. This time ginger ale is used as a mixer, while lime juice and sugar provide the sweet and sour ingredients.

½ lime, peeled and cut into 4 wedges
   (see page 23)
2 measures pineapple juice
1 measure white rum
1 teaspoon caster sugar
dry ginger ale, to top up
lime wheel (see page 23), to decorate

Put the lime wedges, pineapple juice, rum and sugar into a blender and blend on high speed until smooth. Pour into a hurricane glass or large wine goblet and top up with dry ginger ale. Decorate with a lime wheel and serve.

Rum Refashioned
The depth of flavour of aged rum makes it perfect as the main ingredient of this cocktail. Sugar adds a sweet character that is balanced out by the addition of Angostura bitters.

1 brown sugar cube
4 dashes Angostura bitters
ice cubes
2 measures aged rum, such as Havana
   Club 7-year-old
1 dash sugar syrup, or to taste
   (see page 22)
lime rind twist (see page 24),
   to decorate

Put the sugar cube into a rocks (old-fashioned) glass, then splash over the bitters, add 2 ice cubes and stir. Pour over a quarter of the rum, add 2 more ice cubes and stir. Continue building and stirring with the rum and ice cubes, then add sugar syrup to taste. Decorate with a lime rind twist and serve.

Almond Cigar
This award-winning cocktail was invented by one of the owners of Bugsy's in Prague, Czech Republic, a bar famed throughout Eastern Europe.

2 measures golden rum, such as Havana
   Club 3-year-old
1 measure lime cordial
1 measure amaretto
cinnamon stick and lime rind twist
   (see page 24), to decorate

Put all the ingredients into a chilled cocktail shaker and shake well. Pour into a chilled Martini (cocktail) glass. Decorate with a cinnamon stick and lime rind twist and serve.

Spiced Sidecar
Morgan Spiced Rum has a mellow spicy flavour that tastes especially good when enhanced with orange and lemon in this cocktail.

ice cubes
freshly squeezed juice of ½ lemon
1 measure Morgan Spiced Rum
1 measure brandy
1 measure Cointreau
lemon and orange rind twists
   (see page 24), to decorate

Half-fill a cocktail shaker with ice cubes and fill a rocks (old-fashioned) glass with ice cubes. Add all the remaining ingredients to the shaker and shake until a frost forms on the outside of the shaker. Strain over the ice in the glass. Decorate with lemon and orange rind twists and serve.

Berlin Blonde
Double cream and ground cinnamon turn this drink into a delicious liquid dessert.

ice cubes
1 measure dark rum
1 measure Cointreau
1 measure double cream
ground cinnamon, to decorate

Half-fill a cocktail shaker with ice cubes. Add all the remaining ingredients and shake until a frost forms on the outside of the shaker. Fine or double strain (see page 11) into a chilled Martini (cocktail) glass. Decorate with a sprinkling of cinnamon and serve. ▲

Frozen Mango Daiquiri
Frozen daiquiris come in all manner of flavours. Mango is a popular choice as the fruit pulp is thick and creamy and blends well with the crushed ice.

1 scoop crushed ice
½ mango, peeled and stoned, plus extra slices to decorate
1 measure freshly squeezed lime juice
1 teaspoon icing sugar
2 measures white rum

Put the crushed ice into a blender. Add all the remaining ingredients and blend on high speed until smooth. Pour into a Margarita (coupette) glass, decorate with mango slices and serve. ▶

Daiquiri
A refreshing white rum, lime and sugar beverage invented in the early 20th century by Jennings S Cox, an American working in the mines of the Cuban town of Daiquirí.

cracked ice cubes (see page 22)
freshly squeezed juice of 2 limes
1 teaspoon sugar syrup (see page 22)
3 measures white rum
lime wheel (see page 23), to decorate

Put plenty of cracked ice into a cocktail shaker. Add all the remaining ingredients and shake until a frost forms on the outside of the shaker. Strain into a chilled Martini (cocktail) glass. Decorate with a lime wheel and serve.

Strawberry and Mint Daiquiri
Strawberries and mint are a match made in heaven. This sweet, thick cocktail should be served ice cold for ultimate enjoyment.

3 strawberries, plus an extra strawberry slice to decorate
1 dash strawberry syrup
6 mint leaves, plus an extra to decorate
ice cubes
2 measures golden rum
2 measures freshly squeezed lime juice

Put the strawberries, strawberry syrup and mint into a cocktail shaker and muddle together (see page 28). Half-fill the shaker with ice cubes. Add the rum and lime juice and shake until a frost forms on the outside of the shaker. Fine or double strain (see page 11) into a chilled Martini (cocktail) glass. Decorate with a strawberry slice and a mint leaf and serve.

Bacardi Cocktail
In 1936, a New York State Supreme Court ruled it illegal to make this cocktail without using Bacardi rum.

ice cubes
2 measures Bacardi white rum
¾ measure freshly squeezed lime juice
½ measure grenadine
lime rind spiral (see page 24),
   to decorate

Half-fill a cocktail shaker with ice cubes. Add all the remaining ingredients and shake until a frost forms on the outside of the shaker. Strain into a chilled Martini (cocktail) glass. Decorate with a lime rind spiral and serve.

Foxy's Millennium Punch
Foxy's is a famous bar in the British Virgin Islands. It was voted as one of the best places to be for the new Millennium – and here's the drink to prove it.

ice cubes
1½ measures white rum
1 measure dark rum
2 measures cranberry juice
2 measures guava juice
½ measure freshly squeezed lime juice
pineapple slices and lime wheels
   (see page 23), to decorate

Put some ice cubes into a large highball glass. Build all the remaining ingredients, one by one in order, over the ice and stir. Decorate with pineapple slices and lime wheels and serve.

Red Rum
Redcurrants and sloe gin give this cocktail its colourful hue. Vanilla syrup helps to take the edge away from the piquant berries.

small handful of redcurrants, plus an
   extra string to decorate
½ measure sloe gin
ice cubes
2 measures Bacardi 8-year-old rum
½ measure freshly squeezed lemon juice
½ measure vanilla syrup

Put the redcurrants and sloe gin into a cocktail shaker and muddle together (see page 28). Half-fill the shaker with ice cubes. Add all the remaining ingredients and shake until a frost forms on the outside of the shaker. Fine or double strain (see page 11) into a chilled Martini (cocktail) glass. Decorate with a string of redcurrants and serve.

Discovery Bay
A strong rum cocktail that's tempered by lime juice and sugar. The bitters and curaçao add a depth to the drink without detracting from the rum base.

4–5 ice cubes
3 drops Angostura bitters
freshly squeezed juice of ½ lime
1 teaspoon orange or blue curaçao
1 teaspoon sugar syrup (see page 22)
3 measures golden or dark rum
lime twist (see page 24), to decorate

Put the ice cubes into a cocktail shaker and shake over the bitters. Add all the remaining ingredients and shake until a frost forms on the outside of the shaker. Strain into a rocks (old-fashioned) glass. Decorate with a lime twist and serve. ▲

El Dorado
Advocaat is a Dutch liqueur that's made from brandy, sugar and egg yolks. Here, it blends with rum and crème de cacao for a smooth, creamy cocktail.

4–5 ice cubes
1 measure white rum
1 measure advocaat
1 measure white crème de cacao
2 teaspoons grated coconut, plus extra
**   to decorate**

Put the ice cubes into a cocktail shaker. Add all the remaining ingredients and shake until a frost forms on the outside of the shaker. Strain into a chilled Martini (cocktail) glass, decorate with a sprinkling of grated coconut and serve. ◄

Bolero
This is a popular cocktail that contains a lot of spirits. The flavours aren't diluted with mixers so sip this one cautiously.

ice cubes
1½ measures white rum
¾ measure apple brandy
several drops sweet vermouth
lemon rind twist (see page 24),
**   to decorate**

Half-fill a cocktail shaker with ice cubes. Add all the remaining ingredients and shake until a frost forms on the outside of the shaker. Strain into a rocks (old-fashioned) glass. Add some ice cubes. Squeeze a lemon rind twist over the drink, drop it in and serve.

Tobago
Named after the Caribbean island, this simple combination of rum, gin and freshly squeezed lime juice is given an exotic twist with the addition of guava syrup.

crushed ice
½ measure low-proof rum
½ measure gin
1 teaspoon freshly squeezed lime juice
1 teaspoon guava syrup

Fill a rocks (old-fashioned) glass with crushed ice. Put all the remaining ingredients into a chilled cocktail shaker and shake well. Pour over the ice in the glass and serve.

Yellow Bird
Galliano is a sweet liqueur with a lovely yellow colour. It's made from various spices and herbs including vanilla, anise and peppercorns.

ice cubes
1½ measures white rum
1 measure freshly squeezed lime juice
½ measure Galliano
½ measure triple sec

Half-fill a cocktail shaker with ice cubes. Add all the remaining ingredients and shake until a frost forms on the outside of the shaker. Strain into a chilled Martini (cocktail) glass and serve.

Spiced Berry
Warming spiced rum is given a fruit burst with lime and raspberry in this complex-flavoured blend.

ice cubes
1 measure Morgan Spiced Rum
1 dash freshly squeezed lime juice
1 dash raspberry purée
1 dash sugar syrup (see page 22)

Half-fill a cocktail shaker with ice cubes. Add all the remaining ingredients and shake briefly to mix. Strain into a chilled shot glass and serve.

Bossanova
The refreshing blend of apple and lime juices creates a long drink with an ample helping of alcohol.

ice cubes
2 measures white rum
½ measure Galliano
½ measure apricot brandy
4 measures pressed apple juice
1 measure freshly squeezed lime juice
½ measure sugar syrup (see page 22)
lime wedges (see page 23), split,
   to decorate

Half-fill a cocktail shaker with ice cubes and fill a highball glass with ice cubes. Add all the remaining ingredients to the shaker and shake until a frost forms on the outside of the shaker. Strain over the ice in the glass. Decorate with split lime wedges and serve with long straws.

The Boadas Cocktail

Dubonnet is available in red and white varieties and it is often served as an aperitif. The rich colour of red Dubonnet is used here to create a glamorous drink that is finished with a cherry.

1 measure white rum
1 measure red Dubonnet
1 measure orange curaçao
maraschino cherry, to decorate

Put all the ingredients into a mixing glass. Stir well and pour into a small Martini (cocktail) glass. Decorate with a maraschino cherry and serve. ▲

Gin

Gin Sling
*This popular relative of the **Singapore Sling** is a deliciously refreshing long drink. It has a piquant flavour courtesy of the lemon juice so it's a good choice for hot days.*

4–5 ice cubes
freshly squeezed juice of ½ lemon
1 measure cherry brandy
3 measures gin
soda water, to top up
maraschino cherry and a lemon slice,
   to decorate

Put the ice cubes into a cocktail shaker. Add the lemon juice, cherry brandy and gin and shake until a frost forms on the outside of the shaker. Pour, without straining, into a highball glass and top up with soda water. Decorate with a maraschino cherry and a lemon slice and serve with straws. ▶

Gin and Tonic
An all-time classic, which, owing to the quinine originally included in tonic water, was particularly popular in Britain's tropical colonies as an anti-malarial medicine.

ice cubes
2 measures gin
4 measures tonic water
2 lime wedges (see page 23), to decorate

Fill a highball glass with ice cubes. Pour over the gin and then the tonic. Decorate with the lime wedges and serve.

Tom Collins
This is the best-known of the Collins group of long drinks that first rose to popularity during the First World War, originally made with Old Tom, a slightly sweetened gin.

2 measures gin
1½ teaspoons freshly squeezed
   lemon juice
1 teaspoon sugar syrup (see page 22)
ice cubes
soda water, to top up
lemon wheel (see page 23), to decorate

Put the gin, lemon juice and sugar syrup into a highball glass, stir well and fill up with ice cubes. Top up with soda water. Decorate with a lemon wheel and serve.

Cherry Julep

There are many julep cocktails and this is a rich, colourful version. The word itself derives from julab, which is a Persian word meaning rosewater.

3–4 ice cubes
crushed ice
freshly squeezed juice of ½ lemon
1 teaspoon sugar syrup (see page 22)
1 teaspoon grenadine
1 measure cherry brandy
1 measure sloe gin
2 measures gin
lemon rind spirals (see page 24),
    to decorate

Put the ice cubes into a cocktail shaker and fill a highball glass with crushed ice. Add all the remaining ingredients to the shaker and shake until a frost forms on the outside of the shaker. Strain over the ice in the glass. Decorate with lemon rind spirals and serve.

Hong Kong Sling

Lychees – whole, puréed and in the form of a liqueur – give this cocktail its Asian name and flavour. It's easy to find the fruit in supermarkets these days.

ice cubes
1½ measures gin
½ measure lychee liqueur
1 measure lychee purée
1 measure freshly squeezed lemon juice
½ measure sugar syrup (see page 22)
soda water, to top up
whole lychee, unpeeled, to decorate

Half-fill a cocktail shaker with ice cubes and put some ice cubes into a highball glass. Add the gin, lychee liqueur, lychee purée, lemon juice and sugar syrup to the shaker and shake until a frost forms on the outside of the shaker. Strain over the ice in the glass. Stir and top up with soda water. Decorate with a lychee and serve with long straws.

Pink Gin

Angostura bitters, originally intended for medical use, were put into glasses of gin by the Royal Navy, and thus pink gin was invented.

1–4 dashes Angostura bitters
1 measure gin
iced water, to top up

Shake the bitters into a Martini (cocktail) glass and swirl around to coat the inside of the glass. Add the gin and top up with iced water to taste, then serve.

Berry Collins

Muddled fresh summer berries add an exotic flavour to a classic Collins, making it the perfect cocktail for a long, sunny afternoon.

4 raspberries, plus extra to decorate
4 blueberries
1 dash strawberry syrup
crushed ice
2 measures gin
2 teaspoons freshly squeezed
   lemon juice
sugar syrup (see page 22), to taste
soda water, to top up

Put the berries and strawberry syrup into a highball glass and muddle together (see page 28). Fill the glass with crushed ice. Pour over the gin, lemon juice and sugar syrup. Stir well and top up with soda water. Decorate with the extra raspberries and serve. ▲

Negroni
An American GI called Negroni stationed in Italy during the Second World War wanted an extra kick to his Americano, so the bartender added gin and this cocktail was born.

ice cubes
1 measure Plymouth Gin
1 measure Campari
1 measure red vermouth
soda water, to top up (optional)
orange slice, to decorate

Put some ice cubes into a mixing glass and fill a rocks (old-fashioned) glass with ice cubes. Add the gin, Campari and vermouth to the mixing glass, stir briefly to mix and strain over the ice in the glass. Top up with soda water, if you like. Decorate with an orange slice and serve. ▶

Bronx
There are three types of vermouth – dry, sweet and white. It is essentially a fortified wine to which a mixture of herbs and spices are added.

ice cubes, cracked (see page 22)
1 measure gin
1 measure sweet vermouth
1 measure dry vermouth
2 measures freshly squeezed
   orange juice

Put a small glassful of cracked ice into a cocktail shaker. Add all the remaining ingredients, shake briefly to mix and pour into a Martini (cocktail) glass – you can strain the drink if you like.

Gin Garden
This is the perfect cocktail for imbibing on a steamy summer's day with its cleansing cucumber and elderflower cordial. Use freshly pressed apple juice, if possible.

¼ cucumber, peeled and chopped, plus
   extra peeled slices to decorate
½ measure elderflower cordial
ice cubes
2 measures gin
1 measure pressed apple juice

Put the cucumber and elderflower cordial into a cocktail shaker and muddle together (see page 28). Half-fill the shaker with ice cubes. Add the gin and apple juice and shake until a frost forms on the outside of the shaker. Fine or double strain (see page 11) into a chilled Martini (cocktail) glass. Decorate with peeled cucumber slices and serve.

Salty Dog

*A Salty Dog can also be made with vodka. Sometimes the rim of the glass is frosted with salt, like a **Margarita**.*

2–3 ice cubes

pinch of salt

1 measure gin

2–2½ measures freshly squeezed
   grapefruit juice

orange wheel (see page 23), to decorate

Put the ice cubes into a rocks (old-fashioned) glass. Add the salt, pour over the gin and grapefruit juice and stir gently. Decorate with an orange wheel and serve.

Abbey Road

The combination of ginger, lemon and mint results in an unusual flavour that's both warming and zingy.

6 mint leaves

1 piece crystallized ginger

½ measure freshly squeezed lemon juice

ice cubes

crushed ice

2 measures gin

1 measure apple juice

lemon wedge (see page 23), to decorate

Put the mint, ginger and lemon juice into a cocktail shaker and muddle together (see page 28). Half-fill the shaker with ice cubes and put some crushed ice into a rocks (old-fashioned) glass. Add the gin and apple juice to the shaker and shake until a frost forms on the outside of the shaker. Strain over the ice in the glass. Decorate with a lemon wedge and serve.

Monkey Gland

Pomegranate flavour from the grenadine and aniseed from the Pernod give this gin and orange base a real kick.

3–4 ice cubes

1 measure freshly squeezed orange juice

2 measures gin

3 dashes Pernod

3 dashes grenadine

Put the ice cubes into a cocktail shaker. Add all the remaining ingredients and shake until a frost forms on the outside of the shaker. Strain into a chilled Martini (cocktail) glass and serve.

Orange Blossom
This is a cocktail from the American Prohibition years, when it was also sometimes known as an Adirondack. The orange juice could disguise a hearty slug of rotgut gin.

2–3 ice cubes
1 measure gin
1 measure sweet vermouth
1 measure freshly squeezed orange juice
orange wheel (see page 23), to decorate

Put the ice cubes into a highball glass. Put all the remaining ingredients into a chilled cocktail shaker and shake briefly to mix. Pour over the ice in the glass. Decorate with an orange wheel and serve. ▲

Luigi
Grenadine is a red, non-alcoholic syrup that's made from pomegranates. As well as imparting a lovely rich colour to drinks, it adds a fruity flavour.

4–5 ice cubes
1 measure freshly squeezed orange juice
1 measure dry vermouth
½ measure Cointreau
1 measure grenadine
2 measures gin
orange rind knot, to decorate

Put the ice cubes into a mixing glass. Add all the remaining ingredients, stir vigorously and strain into a chilled Martini (cocktail) glass. Decorate with an orange rind knot and serve. ▸

Opera
There's a colourful theme in this cocktail with the gorgeous red Dubonnet and orange curaçao. An orange rind spiral completes the look.

4–5 ice cubes
1 measure red Dubonnet
½ measure orange curaçao
2 measures gin
orange rind spiral (see page 24),
   to decorate

Put the ice cubes into a mixing glass. Pour over all the remaining ingredients, stir evenly and strain into a chilled Martini (cocktail) glass. Decorate with an orange rind spiral and serve.

White Lady
Another citrus-inspired drink but this time the flavour comes from Cointreau, the orange liqueur that's produced in Angers, France.

ice cubes
1 measure gin
1 measure Cointreau
1 measure freshly squeezed lemon juice
lemon rind twist (see page 24),
   to decorate

Half-fill a cocktail shaker with ice cubes. Add all the remaining ingredients and shake until a frost forms on the outside of the shaker. Strain into a chilled Martini (cocktail) glass. Decorate with a lemon rind twist and serve.

Gin Fizz *Created in the mid-19th century, fizzes are long, gently sparkling drinks, traditionally made with a spirit, lemon juice and sugar, and topped up with a fizzy drink.*

ice cubes
2 measures Plymouth Gin
1 measure freshly squeezed lemon juice
2–3 dashes sugar syrup (see page 22)
¼ egg white, beaten
soda water, to top up
lemon wheels (see page 23) and mint
   sprig, to decorate

Half-fill a cocktail shaker with ice cubes. Add the gin, lemon juice, sugar syrup and egg white and shake briefly to mix. Strain into a highball glass and top up with soda water. Decorate with lemon wheels and a mint sprig and serve.

Gibson *The Martini purist mixes their tipple with an almost religious fervour. So if you prefer a cocktail onion in your drink rather than an olive, its a **Gibson**, not a Martini.*

5–6 ice cubes
½ measure dry vermouth
3 measures gin
cocktail onion, to decorate

Put the ice cubes into a mixing glass. Pour over the vermouth and gin and stir (never shake) vigorously and evenly without splashing. Strain into a chilled Martini (cocktail) glass. Decorate with a cocktail onion and serve.

Gin Tropical *The 'tropical' part of this cocktail's name comes from the addition of passion fruit juice. This adds a sweet, exotic flavour.*

4–6 ice cubes
1½ measures gin
1 measure freshly squeezed lemon juice
1 measure passion fruit juice
½ measure freshly squeezed
   orange juice
soda water, to top up
orange rind spiral (see page 24),
   to decorate

Put half the ice cubes into a cocktail shaker and put the remaining half into a rocks (old-fashioned) glass. Add the gin, lemon juice, passion fruit juice and orange juice to the shaker and shake until a frost forms on the outside of the shaker. Strain over the ice in the glass. Top up with soda water and stir gently. Decorate with an orange rind spiral and serve.

Clover Club
The egg white and sugar syrup give this cocktail a lovely pale, frothy appearance. Lime juice adds a sour bite.

4–5 ice cubes
freshly squeezed juice of 1 lime
½ teaspoon sugar syrup (see page 22)
1 egg white
3 measures gin
lime rind, to decorate

Put the ice cubes into a cocktail shaker. Add all the remaining ingredients and shake until a frost forms on the outside of the shaker. Strain into a highball glass. Decorate with lime rind and serve. ▲

Mbolero
A popular ingredient in a number of cocktails, orange bitters are produced from the rinds of unripe oranges. Here, the bitters flavour a simple gin-based drink.

2 lime wedges (see page 23)
ice cubes
2 measures gin
6 mint leaves
6 drops orange bitters
1 dash sugar syrup (see page 22)
mint sprig, to decorate

Squeeze the lime wedges into a cocktail shaker. Half-fill the shaker with ice cubes. Add all the remaining ingredients and shake until a frost forms on the outside of the shaker. Fine or double strain (see page 11) into a chilled Martini (cocktail) glass, decorate with a mint sprig and serve. ◄

Gin Cup
This is a really simple combination of gin, mint and freshly squeezed lemon juice. It's a pure-tasting cocktail for ultimate refreshment.

3 mint sprigs, plus extra to decorate
1 teaspoon sugar syrup (see page 22)
ice cubes, cracked (see page 22)
freshly squeezed juice of ½ lemon
3 measures gin

Put the mint and sugar syrup into a rocks (old-fashioned) glass and muddle together (see page 28). Fill the glass with cracked ice, add the lemon juice and gin and stir until a frost begins to form on the outside of the glass. Decorate with extra mint sprigs and serve.

Dry Martini
This most famous cocktail of all was invented at the Knickerbocker Hotel in New York in 1910. Lemon rind is sometimes used as a decoration instead of a green olive.

5–6 ice cubes
½ measure dry vermouth
3 measures gin
green olive, to decorate

Put the ice cubes into a mixing glass. Pour over the vermouth and gin and stir (never shake) vigorously and evenly without splashing. Strain into a chilled Martini (cocktail) glass. Decorate with a green olive and serve.

Smoky

A single measure of sloe gin adds an interesting extra dimension to a traditional Martini to create this colourful cocktail.

ice cubes
¼ measure dry vermouth
2 measures gin
1 measure sloe gin
5 drops orange bitters
orange rind, to decorate

Put some ice cubes into a mixing glass. Pour over the vermouth and stir until the ice cubes are well coated. Add all the remaining ingredients, stir well and strain into a chilled Martini (cocktail) glass. Decorate with orange rind and serve. ▲

Ginger Tom

This cocktail owes its name to the ginger syrup. This is easy to make yourself or you can buy it ready made.

ice cubes
1½ measures gin
1 measure Cointreau
1 dash freshly squeezed lime juice
1 dash sweetened ginger syrup
1½ measures cranberry juice
lime rind spiral (see page 24),
    to decorate

Half-fill a cocktail shaker with ice cubes. Add all the remaining ingredients and shake briefly to mix. Strain into a chilled Martini (cocktail) glass. Decorate with a lime rind spiral and serve.

Vesper

Lillet is a French aperitif made from a blend of wine, liqueurs, fruit and herbs. It also comes in a red variety.

ice cubes
3 measures gin
1 measure vodka
½ measure Lillet Blanc
lemon rind twist (see page 24),
    to decorate

Half-fill a cocktail shaker with ice cubes. Add the gin, vodka and Lillet and shake until a frost forms on the outside of the shaker. Strain into a chilled Martini (cocktail) glass. Decorate with a lemon rind twist and serve.

Opal Martini

In this vibrantly fruity cocktail, the taste of the fresh orange juice is emphasized by the intense and powerful orange flavour of the Cointreau liqueur.

ice cubes
2 measures gin
1 measure Cointreau
2 measures freshly squeezed
    orange juice
orange rind twist (see page 24),
    to decorate

Half-fill a cocktail shaker with ice cubes. Add all the remaining ingredients and shake until a frost forms on the outside of the shaker. Strain into a chilled Martini (cocktail) glass. Drape a long twist of orange rind in the drink and around the stem of the glass in a swirl, then serve.

Aviation

Maraschino cherries are preserved in alcohol and then soaked in sugar and food colourings to give them their distinctive flavour. They're an essential storecupboard item for budding mixologists.

ice cubes
2 measures gin
½ measure maraschino
½ measure freshly squeezed lemon juice
maraschino cherry, to decorate

Half-fill a cocktail shaker with ice cubes. Add all the remaining ingredients and shake until a frost forms on the outside of the shaker. Fine or double strain (see page 11) into a chilled Martini (cocktail) glass. Decorate with a maraschino cherry and serve. ▸

French '75

*'It hits the spot with remarkable precision', wrote a cocktail book 80 years ago about the **French '75**. It still does!*

ice cubes, cracked (see page 22)
1 measure gin
freshly squeezed juice of ½ lemon
1 teaspoon caster sugar
chilled Champagne or sparkling dry
    white wine, to top up
orange wheel (see page 23), to decorate

Half-fill a highball glass with cracked ice. Add the gin, lemon juice and sugar and stir well. Top up with chilled Champagne or sparkling dry white wine. Decorate with an orange wheel and serve.

French '66

*Orange bitters replace lemon juice and sloe gin is used instead of regular, in this variation of the **French '75**. Perfect as an aperitif.*

1 white sugar cube
6 dashes orange bitters
1 measure sloe gin
freshly squeezed juice of ¼ lemon
chilled Champagne, to top up
lemon rind spiral (see page 24),
    to decorate

Soak the sugar in the bitters, then drop it into a Champagne flute. Add the sloe gin and lemon juice and stir. Top up with chilled Champagne. Decorate with a lemon rind spiral and serve.

Whisky

Big Buff
*A fruity version of the **Rhett Butler**, containing a mixture of berries. Buffalo Trace Bourbon has a delicious vanilla character.*

1 strawberry
3 raspberries
3 blueberries
2 teaspoons Chambord
ice cubes
1 dash freshly squeezed lime juice
2 measures Buffalo Trace
 Bourbon Whiskey
3 measures cranberry juice

Put the mixed berries and the Chambord into a cocktail shaker and muddle together (see page 28). Half-fill the shaker with ice cubes. Add all the remaining ingredients and shake until a frost forms on the outside of the shaker. Pour, without straining, into a highball glass and serve. ▸

Mint Julep
This is the ultimate cocktail of America's Deep South. The earliest written reference dates this aperitif back to 1803.

10 mint leaves, plus an extra sprig
 to decorate
1 teaspoon sugar syrup (see page 22)
4 dashes Angostura bitters
crushed ice
2 measures bourbon

Put the mint leaves, sugar syrup and bitters into a highball glass and muddle together (see page 28). Fill the glass with crushed ice. Pour over the bourbon and stir well. Decorate with a mint sprig and serve.

Rickey
Whisky, lime juice, soda and a lime rind twist are all it takes to prepare this simple but delicious cocktail.

4–5 ice cubes
1½ measures whisky
1½ measures freshly squeezed lime juice
soda water, to top up
lime rind twist (see page 24),
 to decorate

Put the ice cubes into a highball glass. Pour over the whisky and lime juice. Top up with soda water and stir. Decorate with a lime rind twist and serve.

Bourbon Peach Smash
The character of this drink comes from the texture of the muddled fruit and the flecks of bright green mint.

6 mint leaves
3 peach slices
3 lemon slices
2 teaspoons caster sugar
ice cubes
crushed ice
2 measures bourbon
lemon wedge (see page 23), to decorate

Put the mint leaves, peach and lemon slices and sugar into a cocktail shaker and muddle together (see page 28). Half-fill the shaker with ice cubes and put some crushed ice into a rocks (old-fashioned) glass. Add the bourbon to the shaker and shake until a frost forms on the outside of the shaker. Strain over the ice in the glass. Decorate with a lemon wedge and serve. ▲

Rhett Butler
A dry concoction combining bourbon and cranberry juice together with a hint of lime.

ice cubes
2 measures bourbon
4 measures cranberry juice
2 tablespoons sugar syrup (see page 22)
1 tablespoon freshly squeezed lime juice
lime wheels (see page 23), to decorate

Half-fill a cocktail shaker with ice cubes and fill a rocks (old-fashioned) glass with ice cubes. Add all the remaining ingredients to the shaker and shake until a frost forms on the outside of the shaker. Strain over the ice in the glass. Decorate with lime wheels and serve.

A Kiwi in Tennessee
This is a refreshing drink for whiskey lovers – the kiwifruit imparts an intense fruity flavour.

½ kiwifruit, peeled, plus extra slices
    to decorate
ice cubes
2 measures Jack Daniel's
    Tennessee Whiskey
1 measure kiwifruit schnapps
1 measure freshly squeezed lemon juice
lemonade, to top up

Put the kiwifruit into a cocktail shaker and muddle (see page 28). Half-fill the shaker with ice cubes and fill a highball glass with ice cubes. Add the whiskey, schnapps and lemon juice to the shaker and shake until a frost forms on the outside of the shaker. Strain over the ice in the glass. Stir and top up with lemonade. Decorate with kiwifruit slices and serve.

Bobby Burns
Bénédictine is a liqueur made from brandy and over 20 spices and plant extracts. It dates from the 16th century, when it was created by a Bénédictine monk in Normandy.

4–5 ice cubes
1 measure Scotch whisky
1 measure dry vermouth
1 tablespoon Bénédictine
lemon rind spiral (see page 24),
    to decorate

Put the ice cubes into a cocktail shaker. Add all the remaining ingredients and shake until a frost forms on the outside of the shaker. Strain into a chilled Martini (cocktail) glass. Decorate with a lemon rind spiral and serve.

Eclipse

There are a lot of ingredients in this drink but it's well worth the extra effort. The dry, sharp flavours of the cranberry juice and lime juice are complemented by sweet raspberry purée.

ice cubes

crushed ice

2 measures Jack Daniel's
   Tennessee Whiskey

½ measure Chambord

½ measure freshly squeezed lime juice

1 dash sugar syrup (see page 22)

1 measure cranberry juice

1 measure raspberry purée

raspberry and a lime wedge (see page
   23), to decorate

Half-fill a cocktail shaker with ice cubes and put some crushed ice into a large highball glass. Add all the remaining ingredients to the shaker and shake until a frost forms on the outside of the shaker. Strain over the ice in the glass. Decorate with a raspberry and a lime wedge and serve with long straws. ▶

Lynchburg Lemonade

A classic based on Jack Daniel's 'sour mash' Tennessee Whiskey, and created for the Jack Daniel's distillery in Lynchburg, Tennessee.

ice cubes

1½ measures Jack Daniel's
   Tennessee Whiskey

1 measure Cointreau

1 measure freshly squeezed lemon juice

lemonade, to top up

lemon wheels (see page 23), to decorate

Half-fill a cocktail shaker with ice cubes and fill a highball glass with ice cubes. Add the whiskey, Cointreau and lemon juice to the shaker and shake until a frost forms on the outside of the shaker. Strain over the ice in the glass. Top up with lemonade and stir. Decorate with lemon wheels and serve.

Vanilla Daisy

Vanilla syrup and grenadine add a smooth, sweet note to this bourbon-based Daisy – a group of refreshing iced drinks ideal for the summertime.

crushed ice

2 measures bourbon

1 measure freshly squeezed lemon juice

1 measure vanilla syrup

1 teaspoon grenadine

2 maraschino cherries, to decorate

Put some crushed ice into a cocktail shaker and fill a rocks (old-fashioned) glass with crushed ice. Add the bourbon, lemon juice and vanilla syrup to the shaker and shake until a frost forms on the outside of the shaker. Strain over the ice in the glass. Drizzle the grenadine through the drink. Decorate with the maraschino cherries and serve.

Nerida *A glamorous version of the classic 'Scotch and dry', this cocktail relies on the character of the whisky to work its magic.*

4–5 ice cubes
juice of ½ lime or lemon
3 measures Scotch whisky
dry ginger ale, to top up
lime or lemon wheels (see page 23),
   to decorate

Put the ice cubes into a cocktail shaker. Add the lime or lemon juice and whisky and shake until a frost forms on the outside of the shaker. Pour, without straining, into a chilled highball glass. Top up with dry ginger ale and stir gently. Decorate with lime or lemon wheels and serve.

Manhattan *This vintage cocktail was reputedly created at New York's Manhattan Club at the request of Sir Winston Churchill's mother, Lady Randolph Churchill, who was hosting a party for a politician.*

ice cubes
2 measures rye whiskey or bourbon
1 measure extra dry vermouth
4 dashes Angostura bitters
maraschino cherry, to decorate

Put some ice cubes into a mixing glass. Add all the remaining ingredients and stir. Strain into a chilled Martini (cocktail) glass. Decorate with a maraschino cherry and serve.

Old-fashioned *Short for 'old-fashioned whiskey cocktail', and with a glass named after it, this is one of those classic cocktails whose authentic recipe is hotly debated.*

2 measures bourbon
ice cubes
1 teaspoon sugar syrup (see page 22)
4 dashes Angostura bitters
orange rind twist (see page 24),
   to decorate

Pour the bourbon into a rocks (old-fashioned) glass and add a few ice cubes. Build the sugar syrup and then the bitters over the ice. Decorate with an orange rind twist and serve.

Algonquin

A blend of sweet and sour, combining pineapple juice and vermouth with rye. Rye whiskey is made almost entirely from rye grain, whereas bourbon is made from maize and other grains.

ice cubes
1 measure pineapple juice
1 measure dry vermouth
2 measures rye whiskey
pineapple leaf (see page 25), to decorate

Half-fill a cocktail shaker with ice cubes. Add all the remaining ingredients and shake until a frost forms on the outside of the shaker. Strain into a chilled Martini (cocktail) glass, decorate with a pineapple leaf and serve. ▲

Ritz Old-fashioned
*The **Old-fashioned** is given a facelift here with the addition of Grand Marnier and lemon juice. A sugar rim completes the new look.*

lightly beaten egg white
caster sugar
3 ice cubes, crushed (see page 22)
1½ measures bourbon
½ measure Grand Marnier
1 dash freshly squeezed lemon juice
1 dash Angostura bitters
2 maraschino cherries and an orange
**   rind twist (see page 24), to decorate**

Moisten the rim of a rocks (old-fashioned) glass with the egg white and frost with the sugar (see page 26). Put the crushed ice into a cocktail shaker. Add all the remaining ingredients and shake briefly to mix. Strain into the glass. Decorate with 2 maraschino cherries and an orange rind twist and serve. ▸

Rusty Nail
An after-dinner drink whose name is probably due to its colour rather than immigrant Scottish bartenders stirring the cocktail with a rusty nail before serving it to their American patrons, as legend has it.

ice cubes
1½ measures Scotch whisky
1 measure Drambuie

Fill a rocks (old-fashioned) glass with ice cubes. Pour over the whisky and Drambuie and serve.

Whisky Mac
A warming slug made with equal measures of Scotch and ginger wine, this is a delicious winter pick-me-up.

3–4 ice cubes
1 measure Scotch whisky
1 measure ginger wine

Put the ice cubes into a rocks (old-fashioned) glass. Pour over the whisky and ginger wine, stir lightly and serve.

Bourbon Fix
Bourbon is an American variety of whisky. It's made from corn, wheat and malted barley and is aged in oak barrels for a minimum of two years.

ice cubes
2 measures bourbon
1 measure morello cherry purée
1 tablespoon freshly squeezed lime juice
2 teaspoons sugar syrup (see page 22)
lime rind spirals (see page 24),
   to decorate

Half-fill a cocktail shaker with ice cubes and fill a rocks (old-fashioned) glass with ice cubes. Add all the remaining ingredients to the shaker and shake briefly to mix. Strain over the ice in the glass. Decorate with lime rind spirals and serve.

Zoom
This is an unusual Martini made with a healthy slug of Scotch. It is served without a decoration so that the malt flavour can shine through.

ice cubes
2 measures blended Scotch whisky
1 teaspoon clear honey
1 measure iced water
1 measure single cream

Half-fill the cocktail shaker with ice cubes. Add all the remaining ingredients and shake until a frost forms on the outside of the shaker. Strain into a rocks (old-fashioned) glass and serve.

Benedict
This strong whisky cocktail includes a measure of Bénédictine. A little ginger ale tempers the alcohol but it's still a hard-hitting drink.

3–4 ice cubes
1 measure Bénédictine
3 measures Scotch whisky
dry ginger ale, to top up

Put the ice cubes into a mixing glass. Pour over the Bénédictine and whisky, stir evenly without splashing and pour, without straining, into a chilled highball glass. Top up with dry ginger ale and serve.

Godfather Sour
Popular variations on this old classic cocktail replace the bourbon with vodka to make a Godmother, and with brandy to make a Godchild.

ice cubes
1½ measures bourbon
1 measure amaretto
1 measure freshly squeezed lemon juice
1 teaspoon sugar syrup (see page 22)
lemon wheels (see page 23), to decorate

Half-fill a cocktail shaker with ice cubes and fill a rocks (old-fashioned) glass with ice cubes. Add all the remaining ingredients to the shaker and shake until a frost forms on the outside of the shaker. Strain over the ice in the glass. Decorate with lemon wheels and serve. ▲

Harlequin
Canadian Club Whisky is aged in white oak, giving it a lighter, smoother taste than most Scotches and bourbons. It works particularly well with sweet vermouth in this elegant cocktail.

5 white grapes, halved
½ measure sweet vermouth
6 dashes orange bitters
crushed ice
2 measures Canadian Club Whisky

Put the grapes, vermouth and bitters into a rocks (old-fashioned) glass. Half-fill the glass with crushed ice and stir well. Add the whisky, top up with crushed ice and serve. ◄

Rattlesnake
Pernod is a variety of pastis, a liquorice-flavoured drink. It's a French brand and is often drunk by diluting with water, which makes the Pernod cloudy.

ice cubes
1½ measures whisky
1 teaspoon freshly squeezed lemon juice
1 teaspoon sugar syrup (see page 22)
1 egg white
few drops Pernod

Put 4–5 ice cubes into a cocktail shaker. Add all the remaining ingredients and shake extremely well. Strain into a rocks (old-fashioned) glass, add more ice cubes and serve.

Irish Coffee
There are lots of variations on this creamy classic, using virtually any liqueur in place of the whiskey.

1 measure Irish whiskey
hot filter coffee
lightly whipped cream
ground coffee, to decorate

Put a bar spoon into a large toddy glass. Add the whiskey, top up with coffee and stir. Heat the cream very slightly and pour into the bowl of the spoon resting on top of the coffee to get a good float. Decorate with a sprinkling of ground coffee and serve.

Tequila

Tijuana Sling
A long drink with an intriguing mixture of flavours – tequila, blackcurrant, lime and ginger.

ice cubes
1¼ measures tequila
¾ measure crème de cassis
¾ measure freshly squeezed lime juice
2 dashes Peychaud's bitters
4 measures ginger ale
blueberries and lime slices, to decorate

Half-fill a cocktail shaker with ice cubes. Add the tequila, crème de cassis, lime juice and bitters and shake until a frost forms on the outside of the shaker. Pour into a highball glass and top up with ginger ale. Decorate with blueberries and lime slices and serve. ▸

Japanese Slipper
Here's another cocktail that includes the classic combination of tequila and lime juice. The addition of Midori gives a sweet dimension to the drink.

4–5 ice cubes
1¼ measures tequila
¾ measure Midori
1¼ measure freshly squeezed lime juice
lime wheel (see page 23), to decorate

Put the ice cubes into a cocktail shaker. Add all the remaining ingredients and shake until a frost forms on the outside of the shaker. Strain into a Martini (cocktail) glass. Decorate with a lime wheel and serve.

Agave Julep
Contrary to popular myth, tequila is made from agave plants, not cacti. Gold tequila is aged longer for a more intense flavour.

8 mint leaves, torn
1 tablespoon sugar syrup (see page 22)
1¼ measures gold tequila
1¼ measures freshly squeezed lime juice
crushed ice
lime wedge (see page 23) and mint
   sprig, to decorate

Put the torn mint leaves and sugar syrup into a highball glass and muddle together (see page 28). Add the tequila and lime juice, fill the glass with crushed ice and stir vigorously. Decorate with a lime wedge and a mint sprig and serve.

Silk Stocking

This is everything that you expect from a sophisticated cocktail – it is smooth, unusual, beautiful to look at and deceptively powerful.

cocoa powder
4–5 ice cubes
¾ measure tequila
¾ measure white crème de cacao
4 measures single cream
2 teaspoons grenadine

Moisten the rim of a chilled Martini (cocktail) glass with water and frost with the cocoa powder (see page 26). Put the ice cubes into a cocktail shaker. Add all the remaining ingredients and shake until a frost forms on the outside of the shaker. Strain into the glass and serve. ▲

Bloody Maria
Tequila replaces vodka in this variation of the classic **Bloody Mary**. *The spicy kick combined with tomato juice and alcohol makes it a popular hangover 'cure'.*

pepper
celery salt
1 lime wedge (see page 23)
ice cubes
1¼ measures tequila
2 teaspoons medium sherry
2 dashes Tabasco sauce
4 dashes Worcestershire sauce
1 tablespoon freshly squeezed lime juice
4 measures tomato juice
cayenne pepper
celery stick, lime wedge (see page 23)
   and basil sprig, to decorate

Mix some pepper and celery salt together on a small saucer. Moisten the rim of a rocks (old-fashioned) glass with the lime wedge, then frost with the pepper and salt mixture (see page 26). Half-fill a cocktail shaker with ice cubes. Add the tequila, sherry, Tabasco sauce, Worcestershire sauce, lime juice, tomato juice and a pinch each of celery salt, pepper and cayenne pepper. Shake until a frost forms on the outside of the shaker and pour into the glass. Decorate with a celery stick, lime wedge and basil sprig and serve.

Tequila Sunrise
This was a popular cocktail during the Prohibition years in the USA, because the orange juice helped to disguise the unpleasant taste of raw alcohol.

5–6 ice cubes
1 measure tequila
4 measures freshly squeezed
   orange juice
2 teaspoons grenadine
star fruit slice and orange wheel
   (see page 23), to decorate

Crack half the ice cubes (see page 22) and put into a cocktail shaker. Put the remaining ice cubes into a highball glass. Add the tequila and orange juice to the shaker and shake briefly to mix. Strain over the ice in the glass. Slowly pour in the grenadine and allow it to settle. Just before serving, stir once. Decorate with a star fruit slice and an orange wheel and serve.

Mexican Mule
The history of José Cuervo can be traced back to 1758 when José Antonio de Cuervo obtained land in Mexico on which to cultivate the agave plants for tequila production.

1 lime, cut into wedges (see page 23)
1 dash sugar syrup (see page 22)
crushed ice
1 measure José Cuervo Gold Tequila
1 measure Kahlúa
ginger ale, to top up

Put the lime wedges and sugar syrup into a highball glass and muddle together (see page 28). Half-fill the glass with crushed ice. Add the tequila and Kahlúa and stir. Top up with ginger ale and serve.

Margarita
The exact origin of this famous drink is unknown. One story tells of a showgirl who was allergic to all alcohol except tequila. She asked a bartender to create her a cocktail with the spirit and the rest is history.

1 lime wedge (see page 23)
rock salt
ice cubes
2 measures Herrudura Reposado Tequila
1 measure freshly squeezed lime juice
1 measure triple sec
lime wheel (see page 23), to decorate

Moisten the rim of a Margarita (coupette) glass with the lime wedge and frost with the salt (see page 26). Half-fill a cocktail shaker with ice cubes. Add all the remaining ingredients and shake until a frost forms on the outside of the shaker. Strain into the glass. Decorate with a lime wheel and serve. ▸

Rude Cosmopolitan
The subtle combination of fruit flavours in this tequila-based Martini belies its alcoholic strength.

ice cubes
1½ measures gold tequila
1 measure Cointreau
1 measure cranberry juice
½ measure freshly squeezed lime juice
flamed orange rind twist (see page 24),
    to decorate

Put the ice cubes into a cocktail shaker. Add all the remaining ingredients and shake until a frost forms on the outside of the shaker. Strain into a chilled Martini (cocktail) glass. Decorate with a flamed orange rind twist and serve.

Grand Margarita
The addition of Grand Marnier brings a new twist to the classic drink by adding a hint of sweetness to the tequila.

1 lime wedge (see page 23), plus an
    extra to decorate
rock salt
ice cubes
1½ measures silver tequila
1 measure Grand Marnier
1 measure freshly squeezed lime juice

Moisten the rim of a Margarita (coupette) glass with the lime wedge and frost with the salt (see page 26). Half-fill a cocktail shaker with ice cubes. Add all the remaining ingredients and shake until a frost forms on the outside of the shaker. Fine or double strain (see page 11) into the glass and decorate with an extra lime wedge.

Strawberry Margarita *A fruity blend of strawberries, ice and tequila – perfect for parties and summer days.*

1 scoop crushed ice
1 measure tequila
1 measure triple sec
1 measure strawberry liqueur
1 measure freshly squeezed lime juice
12 strawberries, plus extra sliced
   strawberries to decorate

Put the crushed ice into a blender. Add all the remaining ingredients and blend on high speed until smooth but slushy. Pour into a chilled Margarita (coupette) glass. Decorate with sliced strawberries and serve. ▶

Cobalt Margarita *It's the addition of blue curaçao that gives this Margarita variation its name. The orange flavour of the Cointreau and the curaçao blend with the grapefruit juice for a citrus hit.*

1 lime wedge (see page 23)
fine sea salt
4–5 ice cubes
1¼ measures tequila
2 teaspoons Cointreau
½ measure blue curaçao
¾ measure freshly squeezed lime juice
¾ measure freshly squeezed
   grapefruit juice
lime rind spiral (see page 24),
   to decorate

Moisten the rim of a chilled Martini (cocktail) glass with the lime wedge and frost with the salt (see page 26). Put the ice cubes into a cocktail shaker. Add all the remaining ingredients and shake until a frost forms on the outside of the shaker. Strain into the glass. Decorate with a lime rind spiral and serve.

Passion Fruit Margarita *Twists on the traditional Margarita work wonderfully with powerfully flavoured fruit. This one uses the exotic tang of passion fruit.*

1 lime wedge (see page 23)
coarse sea salt
ice cubes
1 ripe passion fruit
1½ measures gold tequila
1 measure Cointreau
1 teaspoon passion fruit syrup
1 measure freshly squeezed lime juice
lime wedges (see page 23), to decorate

Moisten the rim of a Margarita (coupette) glass with the lime wedge and frost with the salt (see page 26). Half-fill a cocktail shaker with ice cubes. Halve the passion fruit and scoop out the flesh. Add half to the shaker with all the remaining ingredients and shake until a frost forms on the outside of the shaker. Fine or double strain (see page 11) into the glass. Add the remaining passion fruit flesh, decorate with lime wedges and serve.

Sour Apple
The apple theme runs throughout this drink with apple schnapps, apple juice and an apple wedge decoration.

4–5 ice cubes
1¼ measures tequila
2 teaspoons Cointreau
1 tablespoon apple schnapps
¾ measure freshly squeezed lime juice
¾ measure dry apple juice
Granny Smith apple wedge, to decorate

Put the ice cubes into a cocktail shaker. Add all the remaining ingredients and shake until a frost forms on the outside of the shaker. Strain into a chilled Martini (cocktail) glass. Decorate with a Granny Smith apple wedge and serve.

Forest Fruit
Crème de mûre is a blackberry liqueur, here combined with Chambord, a black raspberry liqueur, and muddled fresh blackberries and raspberries for a lusciously fruity cocktail.

1 lime wedge (see page 23)
soft light brown sugar
2 blackberries, plus an extra to decorate
2 raspberries, plus an extra to decorate
2 teaspoons Chambord
2 teaspoons crème de mûre
1¼ measures tequila
2 teaspoons Cointreau
1¼ measures freshly squeezed
    lemon juice
crushed ice
lemon wheels (see page 23), to decorate

Moisten the rim of a rocks (old-fashioned) glass with the lime wedge and frost with the sugar (see page 26). Drop the berries into the glass and muddle together (see page 28). Stir in the Chambord and crème de mûre. Pour in the tequila, Cointreau and lemon juice, fill with crushed ice and stir gently, lifting the muddled berries from the bottom of the glass. Decorate with lemon wheels and an extra blackberry and raspberry and serve.

Tequini
This is the Mexican equivalent of a Martini, with tequila replacing the gin and the orange bitters adding an exotic tang.

ice cubes
3 dashes orange bitters
3 measures tequila
2 teaspoons dry French vermouth,
    preferably Noilly Prat
3 large black olives, to decorate

Fill a mixing glass with ice cubes. Add the bitters and tequila and stir gently for 10 seconds. Pour the vermouth into a chilled Martini (cocktail) glass, swirl around to coat the inside of the glass and then tip out. Stir the bitters and tequila for a further 10 seconds, then strain into the glass. Decorate with the olives and serve.

Maracuja
Creole Shrub is an attractive golden-coloured rum, which is flavoured with orange rind. It is important to use a really ripe passion fruit for this drink.

4–5 ice cubes
1 ripe passion fruit
1¼ measures gold tequila
1 tablespoon Creole Shrub
¾ measure freshly squeezed lime juice
2 teaspoons Cointreau
1 teaspoon passion fruit syrup
physalis (Cape gooseberry), to decorate

Put the ice cubes into a cocktail shaker. Halve the passion fruit and scoop out the flesh into the shaker. Add all the remaining ingredients and shake until a frost forms on the outside of the shaker. Fine or double strain (see page 11) into a chilled Martini (cocktail) glass. Decorate with a physalis (Cape gooseberry) and serve. ▲

Baja Sour
Amontillado sherry has a distinctive nutty flavour and its easy drinking character has made it a popular choice amongst sherry drinkers. It blends well with the tequila and orange bitters in this recipe.

4–5 ice cubes
1¼ measures gold tequila
2 teaspoons sugar syrup (see page 22)
1¼ measures freshly squeezed
   lemon juice
2 dashes orange bitters
½ egg white
1 tablespoon amontillado sherry
lemon wedge (see page 23) and orange
   rind spiral (see page 24), to decorate

Put the ice cubes into a cocktail shaker. Add the tequila, sugar syrup, lemon juice, bitters and egg white and shake until a frost forms on the outside of the shaker. Pour into a rocks (old-fashioned) glass and drizzle over the sherry. Decorate with a lemon wedge and an orange rind spiral and serve. ◄

El Diablo
Lime and tequila are natural partners and you will find them in many tequila cocktails. Generally, there will also be a sweeter ingredient – here it's ginger ale.

ice cubes
1¼ measures gold tequila
¾ measure freshly squeezed lime juice
2 teaspoons grenadine
4 measures ginger ale
lime wheel (see page 23), to decorate

Fill a highball glass with ice cubes. Pour over the tequila, lime juice and grenadine. Top up with ginger ale and stir gently. Decorate with a lime wheel and serve.

Matador
Packed with pineapple flavour, this is the perfect party cocktail. It's quick and easy to prepare so great for impressing friends.

1 scoop crushed ice
1¼ measures tequila
¾ measure freshly squeezed lime juice
4 measures pineapple juice
1 pineapple chunk, plus an extra wedge
   to decorate
2 teaspoons sugar syrup (see page 22)
lime rind spiral (see page 24),
   to decorate

Put the crushed ice into a blender. Add all the remaining ingredients and blend on high speed for 15 seconds. Pour into a highball glass. Decorate with a pineapple wedge and a lime rind spiral and serve.

Acapulco
Another classic combination of ingredients — rum and coconut — makes its way into this exotic cocktail. It takes its name from the Mexican party town.

ice cubes
1 measure tequila
1 measure white rum
2 measures pineapple juice
1 measure freshly squeezed
   grapefruit juice
1 measure coconut syrup
pineapple wedge, to decorate

Crack 4–5 ice cubes (see page 22) and put into a cocktail shaker. Fill a highball glass with ice cubes. Add all the remaining ingredients to the shaker and shake until a frost forms on the outside of the shaker. Strain over the ice in the glass. Decorate with a pineapple wedge and serve with straws.

Floreciente
The distinctive colour of blood orange comes from a pigment that is more commonly found in red fruits rather than citrus fruit.

1 orange slice
fine sea salt
crushed ice
1¼ measures gold tequila
¾ measure Cointreau
¾ measure freshly squeezed lemon juice
¾ measure freshly squeezed blood
   orange juice
blood orange wedge (see page 23),
   to decorate

Moisten the rim of a rocks (old-fashioned) glass with the orange slice and frost with the salt (see page 26). Fill the glass with crushed ice. Put all the remaining ingredients into a chilled cocktail shaker, shake vigorously for 10 seconds and pour into the glass. Decorate with a blood orange wedge and serve.

40 Licks
Tangy citrus and sweet vanilla provide a real workout for the taste buds in this exotic cocktail, also known as a Vanilla Margarita.

1 lime, cut into 4 wedges (see page 23),
   plus extra lime wedges to decorate
½ measure Madagascan vanilla syrup
crushed ice
1½ measures silver tequila
½ measure Licor 43 (citrus and
   vanilla liqueur)

Put the lime wedges and vanilla syrup into a rocks (old-fashioned) glass and muddle together (see page 28). Add a scoop of crushed ice. Pour over the tequila and Licor 43, stir and add a little more crushed ice. Decorate with lime wedges and serve with short straws.

Pale Original

Ginger syrup and guava juice make a fantastic combination in this drink, their sweetness balanced by the lime juice.

1 scoop crushed ice
2 measures gold tequila
1 measure freshly squeezed lime juice
2 teaspoons ginger syrup
1 measure guava juice
grated lime rind, to decorate

Put the crushed ice into a blender. Add all the remaining ingredients and blend on high speed until slushy. Pour into a large Margarita (coupette) glass. Decorate with grated lime rind and serve. ▲

Brandy

Brandy Alexander
A sweet and creamy after-dinner cocktail with a chocolate aftertaste. Use ice cream instead of cream, blend well and you have a Frozen Alexander.

3 ice cubes, cracked (see page 22)
1 measure brandy
1 measure dark crème de cacao
1 measure single cream
chocolate flake, to decorate

Put the cracked ice into a cocktail shaker. Add all the remaining ingredients and shake until a frost forms on the outside of the shaker. Strain into a chilled Martini (cocktail) glass. Decorate with a sprinkling of chocolate flake and serve. ▸

Jaffa
This cocktail takes its name from a variety of orange. It's not hard to see why with the inclusion of Mandarine Napoléon, orange bitters and chocolate-orange shavings. A real treat for the taste buds.

ice cubes
1 measure brandy
1 measure dark crème de cacao
1 measure single cream
½ measure Mandarine Napoléon
2 dashes orange bitters
orange-flavoured chocolate shavings,
   to decorate

Half-fill a cocktail shaker with ice cubes. Add all the remaining ingredients and shake until a frost forms on the outside of the shaker. Strain into a chilled Martini (cocktail) glass. Decorate with orange-flavoured chocolate shavings and serve.

Brandy Sidecar
This was reputedly created at the Ritz Hotel in Paris during the First World War for one of the bar's regulars, an army captain who travelled in a motorbike sidecar.

ice cubes
1 measure Cointreau
2 measures brandy
1 measure freshly squeezed lemon juice
maraschino cherry and orange rind
   spiral (see page 24), to decorate

Half-fill a cocktail shaker with ice cubes. Add all the remaining ingredients and shake until a frost forms on the outside of the shaker. Strain into a chilled Martini (cocktail) glass. Decorate with a maraschino cherry on a cocktail stick and an orange rind spiral and serve.

Parisien
The flavours of apple and pear are combined in this delicious cocktail, which features Poire William, a clear spirit distilled from Williams dessert pears.

crushed ice
1 measure brandy
½ measure Calvados
1 measure freshly squeezed lemon juice
sugar syrup (see page 22), to taste
½ measure Poire William
apple and pear wheels (see page 23),
   to decorate

Fill a highball glass with crushed ice. Add the brandy, Calvados, lemon juice and sugar syrup to taste. Pour the Poire William over the top. Decorate with apple and pear wheels and serve.

Brandy Flip
A flip is a spirit or wine shaken with egg and sugar until frothy, then dusted with nutmeg. Early flips were warmed by plunging a red-hot poker into the drink.

ice cubes
1 egg
2 measures brandy
1½ teaspoons caster sugar
freshly grated nutmeg, to decorate

Half-fill a cocktail shaker with ice cubes. Add all the remaining ingredients and shake until a frost forms on the outside of the shaker. Strain into a balloon (snifter) glass. Decorate with a little grated nutmeg and serve.

Brandy Fix
Cherry brandy and regular brandy make up the main ingredients of this drink. It's simple to prepare and the addition of lemon juice gives it a tangy finish.

crushed ice
2 teaspoons sugar syrup (see page 22)
1¼ measures freshly squeezed
   lemon juice
½ measure cherry brandy
1 measure brandy
lemon rind spiral (see page 24),
   to decorate

Fill a rocks (old-fashioned) glass with crushed ice. Build all the ingredients, one by one in order, over the ice. Decorate with a lemon rind spiral and serve.

American Beauty
Ruby port gets its name from its distinctive dark red colour. It's a fortified wine with brandy added to stop fermentation at a certain stage so that the alcohol content is higher than regular wine.

4–5 ice cubes
1 measure brandy
1 measure dry vermouth
1 measure freshly squeezed orange juice
1 measure grenadine
1 dash white crème de menthe
2–3 dashes ruby port
maraschino cherries, mint and orange rind spiral (see page 24), to decorate

Put the ice cubes into a cocktail shaker. Add the brandy, vermouth, orange juice, grenadine and crème de menthe and shake until a frost forms on the outside of the shaker. Strain into a Martini (cocktail) glass. Tilt the glass and gently pour in the port so it floats on top. Decorate with maraschino cherries, a mint sprig and an orange rind spiral and serve. ▲

Egg Nog
This traditional wintertime drink contains brandy, rum or bourbon or a combination of all three, plus an egg, sugar and milk or cream.

ice cubes
1 measure brandy
1 measure dark rum
1 egg
1 teaspoon sugar syrup (see page 22)
3 measures full-fat milk
freshly grated nutmeg, to decorate

Half-fill a cocktail shaker with ice cubes. Add the brandy, rum, egg and sugar syrup and shake until a frost forms on the outside of the shaker. Strain into a toddy glass. Pour over the milk. Decorate with a little grated nutmeg and serve. ◄

Brandy Crusta
A Crusta combines a spirit with lemon juice and Angostura bitters and is traditionally served with a lemon rind spiral.

1 lemon wedge (see page 23)
caster sugar
ice cubes
2 measures brandy
½ measure orange curaçao
½ measure maraschino
1 measure freshly squeezed lemon juice
3 dashes Angostura bitters
lemon rind spiral (see page 24),
   to decorate

Moisten the rim of a chilled Martini (cocktail) glass with the lemon wedge and frost with the sugar (see page 26). Half-fill a cocktail shaker with ice cubes. Add all the remaining ingredients and shake until a frost forms on the outside of the shaker. Strain into the glass. Decorate with a lemon rind spiral and serve.

Corpse Reviver
This alcohol-fuelled cocktail is guaranteed to give you a wake-up call, hence its name. Drink these all night at your peril!

3 ice cubes, cracked (see page 22)
2 measures brandy
1 measure Calvados
1 measure sweet vermouth
apple wheels (see page 23), to decorate

Put the cracked ice into a cocktail shaker. Add all the remaining ingredients and shake until a frost forms on the outside of the shaker. Strain into a chilled Martini (cocktail) glass. Decorate with apple wheels and serve.

Nice Pear

Brandy comes in all manner of fruity variations and cocktails will often emphasize this. Pear is the main flavour here.

ice cubes
2 measures brandy
1 measure Poire William
1 measure sweet vermouth
pear slices, to decorate

Half-fill a cocktail shaker with ice cubes. Add all the remaining ingredients and shake until a frost forms on the outside of the shaker. Strain into a chilled Martini (cocktail) glass. Decorate with pear slices and serve. ▲

Between the Sheets
An orange-flavoured drink that delivers a powerful punch. White rum has a much lighter flavour than dark rum, complementing the flavour of the Cointreau and brandy.

ice cubes
½ measure brandy
½ measure white rum
½ measure Cointreau
1 measure freshly squeezed orange juice
orange rind spiral (see page 24),
   to decorate

Half-fill a cocktail shaker with ice cubes. Add all the remaining ingredients and shake briefly to mix. Strain into a chilled Martini (cocktail) glass. Decorate with an orange rind spiral and serve.

Brandy Classic
A colourful cocktail that combines cherry flavours with the brandy. Where no specific brand or variation of spirit is mentioned, choose your favourite.

ice cubes, cracked (see page 22)
1 measure brandy
1 measure blue curaçao
1 measure maraschino
freshly squeezed juice of ½ lemon
lemon wedge (see page 23), to decorate

Put 4–5 cracked ice cubes into a cocktail shaker. Add all the remaining ingredients and shake briefly to mix. Strain into a chilled Martini (cocktail) glass. Add some more cracked ice, decorate with a lemon wedge and serve.

Metropolitan
Equal parts brandy and vermouth are shaken together with sugar syrup and bitters for this classically simple cocktail that is served without decoration.

ice cubes, cracked (see page 22)
1 measure brandy
1 measure sweet vermouth
½ teaspoon sugar syrup (see page 22)
3–4 dashes Angostura bitters

Half-fill a cocktail shaker with cracked ice. Add all the remaining ingredients and shake until a frost forms on the outside of the shaker. Strain into a chilled Martini (cocktail) glass and serve.

Other wines and spirits

Sangria *This classic Spanish punch uses red wine as its foundation. With the addition of chopped fruit and cinnamon, it's like a summertime version of mulled wine.*

Serves 10–12
ice cubes
2 bottles light Spanish red wine, chilled
5 measures brandy
orange, lemon and apple wedges, plus
  orange, lemon and apple wheels
  (see page 23)
cinnamon sticks
about 450 ml (¾ pint) lemonade, chilled

Put some ice cubes into a large jug. Add the wine, brandy, fruit wedges and one cinnamon stick and stir well. When ready to serve, top up with the chilled lemonade and stir. Serve in glasses decorated with orange, lemon and apple wheels and cinnamon sticks. ▶

White Sangria *Here, white wine is used instead of red. The addition of vodka and schnapps dilutes the taste of the wine and adds other flavours to the finished drink.*

Serves 6
2 large glasses dry white wine
2 measures lemon vodka
2 measures peach schnapps
2 measures peach purée
apple, lime, lemon and peach slices
ice cubes
1 measure freshly squeezed lemon juice
1 measure freshly squeezed lime juice
lemonade, to top up

Twelve hours before serving, put the wine, vodka, schnapps, peach purée and fruit slices into a jug and stir to mix. Cover and chill in the refrigerator. Just before serving, add some ice cubes and the fruit juices and top up with lemonade. Serve from the jug into rocks (old-fashioned) glasses.

Cowboy *This sumptuous cocktail will have you licking your lips with its seductive combination of butterscotch schnapps and Baileys.*

1 measure chilled butterscotch schnapps
½ measure Baileys Irish Cream

Pour the schnapps into a chilled shot glass. Float the Baileys over the schnapps (see page 31), then serve.

Riviera Fizz
As its name suggests, sloe gin is flavoured with sloe berries. As well as flavour, these give the gin its distinctive red colour.

ice cubes
1½ measures sloe gin
½ measure freshly squeezed lemon juice
½ measure sugar syrup (see page 22)
chilled Champagne, to top up
lemon rind twist (see page 24),
   to decorate

Half-fill a cocktail shaker with ice cubes. Add the sloe gin, lemon juice and sugar syrup and shake until a frost forms on the outside of the shaker. Strain into a chilled Champagne flute. Top up with chilled Champagne and stir. Decorate with a lemon rind twist and serve.

Cucumber Saketini
This cooling yet deceptively powerful cocktail is a characteristically elegant Japanese speciality.

ice cubes
2½ measures cucumber-infused sake
1½ measures gin
½ measure orange curaçao
peeled cucumber slices, to decorate

Put some ice cubes into a mixing glass. Add all the remaining ingredients and stir together until thoroughly chilled. Strain into a chilled Martini (cocktail) glass. Decorate with peeled cucumber slices and serve.

Champagne Cocktail
There are countless variations of the Champagne Cocktail but many include a sugar cube dissolved with bitters. This creates a lovely visual effect.

1 white sugar cube
1–2 dashes Angostura bitters
1 measure brandy
4 measures chilled Champagne
orange wheel (see page 23), to decorate

Put the sugar cube into a chilled Martini (cocktail) glass or Champagne flute and saturate with the bitters. Add the brandy, then top up with the chilled Champagne. Decorate with an orange wheel and serve.

Singapore Sling
One of the most famous cocktails ever, this was first concocted by the bartender of The Long Bar at Raffles Hotel in Singapore.

ice cubes
1 measure gin
½ measure cherry brandy
¼ measure Cointreau
¼ measure Bénédictine
½ measure grenadine
½ measure freshly squeezed lime juice
5 measures pineapple juice
1 dash Angostura bitters
pineapple wedge and maraschino
   cherry, to decorate

Half-fill a cocktail shaker with ice cubes and put some ice cubes into a highball glass. Add all the remaining ingredients to the shaker and shake until a frost forms on the outside of the shaker. Strain over the ice in the glass. Decorate with a pineapple wedge and a maraschino cherry and serve. ▲

Pisco Sour *First created in the early 1900s, this cocktail came about to render Pisco, a grape brandy often of a low quality, more drinkable with a simple sweet and sour mix.*

ice cubes
2 measures Pisco
1 measure freshly squeezed lemon juice
2 teaspoons caster sugar
1 egg white
dash Angostura bitters

Half-fill a cocktail shaker with ice cubes and fill a large wine goblet with ice cubes. Add the Pisco, lemon juice, sugar and egg white to the shaker and shake until a frost forms on the outside of the shaker. Strain over the ice in the glass. Add the bitters to the drink's frothy head and serve. ◄

Caipirinha *This is by far the most famous of Brazilian cocktails, whose main ingredient is the local liquor, cachaça, of which over 4,000 brands are available.*

1 lime, quartered
2 teaspoons caster sugar
crushed ice
2 measures cachaça

Put the lime quarters and sugar into a rocks (old-fashioned) glass and muddle together (see page 28). Fill the glass with crushed ice and pour over the cachaça. Stir and add more ice as desired.

Goombay Smash *Another cachaça-based drink, this time combined with coconut rum and apricot brandy. It's an eclectic combination of drinks and flavours but it works remarkably well.*

ice cubes
1½ measures coconut rum
1 measure cachaça
½ measure apricot brandy
½ measure freshly squeezed lime juice
4 measures pineapple juice
pineapple slices, maraschino cherries
   and lime rind twist (see page 24),
   to decorate

Half-fill a cocktail shaker with ice cubes and put some ice cubes into a large glass. Add all the remaining ingredients to the shaker and shake until a frost forms on the outside of the shaker. Strain over the ice in the glass. Decorate with pineapple slices, maraschino cherries and a lime rind twist and serve.

Fish House Punch *This punch has been synonymous with the drinking heritage of Philadelphia, Pennsylvania, USA, since the 18th century, and the recipe has remained largely unchanged.*

ice cubes
1 measure brandy
1 measure golden rum
1 measure peach brandy
1 measure freshly squeezed lemon juice
½ measure sugar syrup (see page 22)
1 measure cold tea (English Breakfast)
soda water, to top up
lemon wheel (see page 23), to decorate

Half-fill a cocktail shaker with ice cubes and fill a highball glass with ice cubes. Add the brandy, rum, peach brandy, lemon juice, sugar syrup and tea to the shaker and shake until a frost forms on the outside of the shaker. Fine or double strain (see page 11) over the ice in the glass. Top up with soda water. Decorate with a lemon wheel and serve with long straws.

Buck's Fizz *This can be made in party quantities in a large jug. Use 250 ml (8 fl oz) orange juice to a bottle of Champagne. Allow space for the Champagne to bubble up.*

2½ measures freshly squeezed
   orange juice
7 measures Champagne
orange wheels (see page 23),
   to decorate

Pour the orange juice into a Martini (cocktail) glass and add the Champagne. Decorate with orange wheels and serve.

Kir Royale *One of the more classic ways to drink Champagne, this simple combination of crème de cassis and bubbles makes a simple yet stunning aperitif.*

2 teaspoons crème de cassis
Champagne, to top up

Pour the crème de cassis into a Champagne flute. Top up with Champagne, then serve.

Black Velvet
Here's another popular but simple Champagne cocktail.
People who find Guinness too heavy often enjoy drinking it this way.

5 measures Guinness
5 measures Champagne

Pour the Guinness into a champagne glass.
Carefully add the Champagne, then serve. ▲

Champagne Julep
This is a gorgeous, colourful drink. The fizz of the Champagne moves the muddled mint around the glass.

3 mint sprigs
1 tablespoon sugar syrup (see page 22)
crushed ice
1 measure brandy
Champagne, to top up

Put 2 mint sprigs and the sugar syrup into a highball glass and muddle together (see page 28). Fill the glass with crushed ice, then add the brandy. Top up with Champagne and stir gently. Decorate with a mint sprig, then serve. ▶

Alabama Slammer
This is a drink for serious shot aficionados. There is enough for four people here, so gather round and down them in one.

Serves 4
ice cubes
1 measure Southern Comfort
1 measure vodka
1 measure sloe gin
1 dash freshly squeezed orange juice
4 drops grenadine

Half-fill a cocktail shaker with ice cubes. Add the Southern Comfort, vodka, sloe gin and orange juice and shake briefly to mix. Strain into 4 chilled shot glasses. Add a drop of grenadine to each and serve.

Absinthe Minded
The mighty absinthe is diluted with lemon juice and Chambord here, but don't be lulled into a false sense of security – this is one shot that will knock you for six!

ice cubes
1 measure absinthe
1 dash freshly squeezed lemon juice
1 dash Chambord

Half-fill a cocktail shaker with ice cubes. Add all the remaining ingredients and shake briefly to mix. Strain into a chilled shot glass and serve.

B-52 *This is the classic layered shot that tastes just as good as it looks, with a wonderful warm, sweet flavour.*

½ measure Kahlúa
½ measure Baileys Irish Cream
½ measure Grand Marnier

Using a bar spoon, carefully layer the three ingredients, in order, in a shot glass (see page 31), then serve. ▲

Deaf Knees
Layers of mint, chocolate and orange deliver a powerful kick and an explosion of flavours as you knock back this shot.

½ measure green crème de menthe
½ measure chocolate schnapps
½ measure Grand Marnier

Using a bar spoon, carefully layer the three ingredients, in order, in a shot glass (see page 31), then down it in one gulp!

Flaming Lamborghini
This requires considerable skill on the part of both the bartender and the drinker. Great care must be taken in lighting and extinguishing the sambuca.

1 measure Kahlúa
1 measure sambuca
1 measure blue curaçao
1 measure Baileys Irish Cream

Using a bar spoon, float the sambuca over the Kahlúa in a Martini (cocktail) glass (see page 31). Pour the curaçao and the Baileys into 2 separate shot glasses. Carefully light the surface of the sambuca, then instruct the drinker to take a straw and start to drink from the Martini (cocktail) glass. As the liquid nears the base of the glass, add both the curaçao and the Baileys to extinguish the flame, then instruct the drinker to down the lot!

383
Frangelico is an Italian liqueur that's flavoured with hazelnuts and herbs. It comes in a distinctive bottle that was designed to resemble a monk dressed in a habit.

½ measure Frangelico
1 measure chilled raspberry vodka
1 orange wedge, coated in
  demerara sugar

Pour the Frangelico into a chilled shot glass, then add the vodka. Serve with a sugar-coated orange wedge, to be eaten after the shot is drunk.

Long Island Iced Tea
A very potent brew, supposedly created by Robert 'Rosebud' Butt of the Oak Beach Inn, Hampton Bay.

ice cubes
½ measure vodka
½ measure gin
½ measure white rum
½ measure tequila
½ measure Cointreau
½ measure freshly squeezed lemon juice
cola, to top up
lemon wedge (see page 23), to decorate

Half-fill a cocktail shaker with ice cubes and fill a highball glass with ice cubes. Add the vodka, gin, rum, tequila, Cointreau and lemon juice to the shaker and briefly shake to mix. Strain over the ice in the glass. Top up with cola. Decorate with a lemon wedge and serve. ▸

Parisian Spring Punch
Calvados, Noilly Prat and Champagne give this cocktail its Gallic name. An apple slice highlights the flavour of the brandy and completes this lovely summery drink.

ice cubes
crushed ice
1½ measures Calvados
½ measure freshly squeezed lemon juice
½ measure Noilly Prat
1 teaspoon caster sugar
chilled Champagne, to top up
apple slice, to decorate

Half-fill a cocktail shaker with ice cubes and put some crushed ice into a highball glass. Add the Calvados, lemon juice, Noilly Prat and sugar to the shaker and shake briefly to mix. Strain over the ice in the glass. Top up with chilled Champagne. Decorate with an apple slice and serve.

Pimm's Cocktail
This is more alcoholic than the original, with the addition of gin, but refreshing just the same. Ginger ale adds a delicious spiciness to the drink.

ice cubes
1 measure Pimm's No 1
1 measure gin
2 measures lemonade
2 measures ginger ale
cucumber strips, blueberries and orange
   wheels (see page 23), to decorate

Fill a highball glass with ice cubes. Build all the remaining ingredients, one by one in order, over the ice. Decorate with cucumber strips, blueberries and orange wheels and serve.

Glossary

Absinthe
An infamous spirit steeped with several botanicals, most notably wormwood oil. It was subject to a worldwide ban for many years because of its narcotic effects, which are nowadays attributed more to the abnormally high alcohol content.

Agave
The blue agave plant found in certain areas of Mexico is the raw material from which tequila is made. Contrary to popular belief, tequila is not made from cactus plants.

Amaretto
This almond-flavoured liqueur is actually made from apricot stones. *Amaretto di Saronno* is the original drink, which comes from Saronno in Italy. It is often served as a digestif at the end of a meal and is also used to flavour coffee and ice cream.

Añejo
The Spanish word for 'aged'. It is often used to describe rum and tequila, which both use ageing processes to increase the quality of the product.

Angostura bitters
Although Angostura bitters have a high alcohol content (40%), they are classified as a food additive and used in very small quantities. They are produced in Trinidad to a secret recipe. You will often see the instruction 'add a dash of Angostura bitters' in cocktail recipes.

Aperitif
Anything that is drunk before a meal to stimulate the palate can be considered an aperitif.

Aquavit
A grain-based spirit that is hugely popular in most Scandinavian countries. It is often infused and flavoured.

Armagnac
A French brandy that is made in one of three regions: Tenareze, Haut Armagnac and Bas Armagnac. It has a long history, having been produced since the 15th century. It remains very much a local industry, with many family-run distilleries that have been producing the spirit for several generations.

Baileys Irish Cream
A sweet whiskey and cream, mildly coffee-flavoured liqueur from Ireland, which has proved immensely popular since its debut in the 1970s.

Bénédictine
This is reputed to be the oldest liqueur in the world, formulated by a Bénédictine monk in Normandy, France, in the 16th century. Its secret recipe contains brandy flavoured with various herbs and other aromatics.

Blend
A process in which ingredients are added to a blender and puréed, often with a scoop of crushed ice to chill (see page 33). Never add carbonated liquids to a blender, as the mixture might explode.

Blended whisky
A mixture of neutral grain whisky and single malts. Single malt whiskies are made entirely from malted grain and are more expensive to produce than the blended variety. Blenders work primarily with their sense of

smell to develop the various blends of whisky.

Bourbon
Named after Bourbon County, Kentucky, USA, where it was first made, by law whiskey can only be termed bourbon if produced in the state. Bourbon is distilled primarily from maize, but it also includes other grains.

Brandy
A spirit distilled from fermented fruit. It is usually made by distilling wine, but variations include apple and peach, and its name actually derives from the processes involved in making it rather than the fruit it is based on.

Build
A term used to describe the simplest cocktail-making process, in which a glass is filled with ice and ingredients are poured over, in the correct order and proportion, before the drink is served (see page 32).

Cachaça
Brazil's national spirit, used in the world famous *Caipirinha*. It is distilled from sugar cane and bottled without ageing.

Calvados
This famous apple brandy originates from Normandy in France.

Campari
A bitter Italian aperitif that was developed in the 1860s. The recipe is a closely guarded secret, but the predominant flavouring is orange. The drink has a distinctive red colour, which is obtained from the natural colouring, cochineal.

Chambord
A French liqueur flavoured with black raspberries and honey. It has an illustrious history dating all the way back to the 17th century, and its name is taken from the Château de Chambord in the Loire Valley. The liqueur is still produced in this region and remains a popular French tipple today.

Champagne
A region in France famous for the production of sparkling wine of the same name. Although sparkling wines are produced in many other regions and countries, they are not allowed to bear the name 'Champagne'.

Cointreau
A clear, orange-flavoured liqueur from France.

Crème de cacao
This widely used chocolate-flavoured liqueur is available in both white and dark varieties.

Crème de cassis
A sweet blackcurrant liqueur that is probably best known for being combined with dry white wine to make Kir or chilled Champagne or sparkling dry white wine for *Kir Royale*. It was first produced in Burgundy in the mid-1800s and it is still mainly consumed in France.

Crème de menthe
A sweet, mint-flavoured liqueur, which comes in both green and white (clear) varieties.

Curaçao
Named after a Caribbean island, this liqueur is flavoured with the rind of the bitter oranges that grow there. It is available in several different colours, including orange, blue, yellow, red and green.

Dash
A very small amount of an ingredient added to a cocktail, approximately 5 ml (1 teaspoon). A dash is usually used in relation to ingredients that have a particularly strong flavour and are only required in small quantities, such as bitters, syrups and sauces.

Drambuie
A Scotch whisky liqueur flavoured with heather honey and herbs, reputedly made to a recipe created by Bonnie Prince Charlie himself.

Dubonnet
A blend of fortified wines, flavoured with quinine and herbs, which is available in red and white varieties.

Float
To form a separate layer of liquid on top of another in a drink. This is often achieved by using a bar spoon to pour one liquid ingredient over a second, denser liquid ingredient, as in the technique of layering (see page 31).

Frangelico
An Italian hazelnut- and herb-flavoured liqueur. It was originally produced by monks, hence its monk's habit-shaped bottle with a white cord belt tied around its 'waist'.

Frappé
A chilled drink that is served over finely crushed ice. Frappés are usually served with a straw so that the liquid and ice are consumed together.

Frosting
An effect achieved by coating the rim of a cocktail glass with, usually, sugar or salt (see page 26). The best-known example of this is the *Margarita*.

Galliano
This pale amber-coloured Italian liqueur is flavoured with many different herbs, but aniseed is the predominant taste.

Gin
A grain spirit flavoured with botanicals, most commonly juniper berries. Its dry taste has a refreshing quality, which also makes it a good base for a variety of mixers, tonic water being the most popular, as in *Gin and Tonic*.

Grand Marnier
A popular brandy-based orange-flavoured liqueur from France.

Grappa
A brandy made from the grape skins left over from wine production. Its invention came about almost by accident, as it was originally just an economical way of processing this waste matter. It soon developed a following and was consequently produced on a grand scale.

Grenadine
A sweet, non-alcoholic syrup flavoured with pomegranate. It is bright red in colour and is often used to add a touch of vibrancy to cocktails.

Kahlúa
A coffee-flavoured liqueur produced in Mexico.

Maraschino
A clear liqueur flavoured with wild marasca cherries, including their stones. It also gives its name to the cherries used in cocktails – maraschino cherries – since they were traditionally flavoured with the liqueur, although now they are commonly bottled in a mint-flavoured syrup if green or almond-flavoured syrup if red, with or without stalks.

Midori
A vibrant green-coloured liqueur flavoured with Japanese honeydew melons.

Muddle
A technique in which a blunt tool, known as a muddler (see page 12), is used to mash fruit, herbs and syrups together at the beginning of the cocktail-making process (see page 28). This is done to extract as much flavour as possible from the ingredients by releasing and combining the juices.

On the rocks
A drink served over ice cubes, which enables it to be swiftly chilled and slightly diluted, but at a much slower rate than if crushed ice were used.

Peychaud's bitters
One of the earliest products used to flavour drinks. It was invented in 1793 by Antoine Peychaud in New Orleans, USA. It is still in use in bars today and is made according to the original recipe.

Sake
A Japanese rice wine. Sake is actually a generic term that covers all alcoholic drinks in

Japan and only as an export does the name refer to rice wine in particular. As with grape-based wine, sake literally covers thousands of varieties, qualities and flavours, and people in the West are only able to sample a relatively small proportion of these. In Japan, sake is often drunk warm or hot. Lower-grade sake benefits from being drunk at a hot temperature, as this disguises the coarse flavour.

Sambuca
A dry, aniseed-flavoured Italian liqueur, often served flaming.

Sangria
A traditional Spanish drink that is made with a combination of liqueurs, wine and fruit (see page 140). Many local recipes exist throughout Spain.

Schnapps
German in origin, schnapps is now hugely popular across Scandinavia and in ski resorts around the world. It is a strong, colourless spirit that often has fruit flavourings, such as peach or blackcurrant.

Scotch
The shortened name for Scotch whisky. To be labelled a Scotch whisky legally, the whisky must have been distilled from barley and water in a Scottish distillery. It must also be aged in oak barrels for at least three years.

Shake
The art of mixing and chilling a cocktail in one action (see page 29). The ingredients are all added to a cocktail shaker and shaken vigorously to allow the drink to combine and chill.

Sloe gin
This is made by flavouring gin with sugar and sloes – small hedgerow fruit rather like tiny bitter plums. Traditionally homemade, it can also be bought ready made.

Sours
A cocktail with three parts: a spirit or liqueur, lemon juice and sugar syrup. The ingredients are shaken together in the ratio 2:1:1.

Southern Comfort
An American bourbon-based liqueur flavoured with peaches, oranges and herbs.

Spiral
A decoration made by cutting a long strip of rind from a citrus fruit with a canelle knife and winding it around a cylindrical shape to give it a spiral shape (see page 24). The spiral is either balanced on the side of the glass or it can be added to the drink to give extra flavour as well as decorating the cocktail.

Stir
As a general rule, cocktails featuring transparent ingredients are stirred rather than shaken, in order to maintain the clarity while mixing and chilling them. A bar spoon is used and the drink is usually stirred after it has been built in the glass, although it can also be prepared in a mixing glass, then strained into a serving glass (see page 30).

Straight up
A cocktail that is served without the addition of ice, often in a Martini (cocktail) glass.

Strain

Once a cocktail has been shaken or stirred, it is strained to remove ice and fruit fragments. In standard cocktail shakers, the strainer comes as part of the shaker and is fitted over the shaking tin, while a separate strainer, known as a hawthorne strainer, is used with a Boston shaker (see pages 10–11). When a cocktail must be served absolutely clear, it will require a double strain using a fine strainer (see page 11).

Sugar syrup

Liquid sugar that is used to add sweetness to drinks without the texture of sugar granules, also known as gomme syrup, syrup de gomme or sometimes just gomme. It is made by heating sugar in water until the sugar has completely dissolved (see page 22), or it can be purchased ready made in bottles.

Swizzle stick

This acts as both a stirrer and a decoration, and is often used in cocktails with heavier ingredients, which might otherwise settle on the bottom of the glass. Swizzle sticks are available in a variety of colours and shapes, and can add a fun element to the cocktail.

Tequila

A spirit produced in Mexico from the blue agave plant. The urban myth of the worm in the bottom of the bottle is just that – mezcal is the drink that contains the worm. Tequila is aged for various lengths of time to produce different qualities. Gold tequila and tequila añejo are aged tequilas that can be enjoyed 'straight up' or 'on the rocks' to appreciate the flavours. Younger tequilas, such as silver tequila, are ideal for cocktails.

Triple Sec

A very popular cocktail ingredient that is distilled from curaçao oranges. Unlike many fruit-flavoured liqueurs, triple sec is colourless and its flavour is derived from the rind of the oranges rather than the juice. The name refers to the three steps of the distilling process.

Twist

Similar to a spiral, the twist is used as a decoration and also to add flavour to the drink (see page 24). A long strip of rind is pared from a citrus fruit and it is given a twist in the middle in order to release the oils and add the required flavour to the drink.

Vermouth

Red, rosé or white wine that is fortified and flavoured with herbs and other plant extracts and spices, and is made in both sweet and dry varieties.

Vodka

This spirit takes its name from the Russian and Polish words for 'little water'. It is generally tasteless and odourless, and is distilled from many different ingredients including wheat, rye or potatoes. It is also widely available flavoured with fruit, herbs and spices.

Whisky

A spirit distilled from malted grain and produced all over the world. The 'e' is omitted if the whisky originates from Scotland or Canada. American and Irish varieties are spelt 'whiskey'.

Index

Acknowledgements

Executive Editor Sarah Ford

Editor Leanne Bryan

Executive Art Editor Darren Southern

Design 'ome Design

Production Controller Manjit Sihra

Special photography: © Octopus Publishing Group Ltd / Stephen Conroy

Drinks Stylist Federico Riezzo

Props Stylist Liz Hippisley